I0755093

MEN AND THINGS

AS

I SAW THEM IN EUROPE.

BY KIRWAN.

NEW YORK:
HARPER & BROTHERS, PUBLISHERS,
329 & 331 PEARL STREET,
FRANKLIN SQUARE.
1854.

TO

HIS OWN PEOPLE,

ENDEARED TO HIM BY A MINISTRY OF TWENTY YEARS,
THIS MEMORIAL OF HIS FOREIGN TRAVEL

Is Dedicated

BY THEIR PASTOR.

PREFACE.

WHAT, another book of sketches of men and things in Europe! Yes, verily, another book! But how came you to write it? I will tell you. First, because many of my friends seemed determined that I should write it. Secondly, because I had collected matter enough for a volume during my rambles. Thirdly, I have as good a right to maintain the truth of the proverb, that "of making books there is no end," as any body else. Fourthly, because I saw things with my own eyes, and desired to tell about them in my own way. Fifthly, because I believe I have friends and readers enough to exhaust at least one edition, who are desirous to know who and what I saw, and what I think about them; and I have a wish to gratify them. And, lastly, because I thought I could make some revelations as to religion, morals, and men, that may be of some use to my generation. If these reasons are not satisfactory, the reader has my hearty consent to lay down this volume unread. The loss may be as much his as mine.

I describe things as I saw them; and if my pictures are not true, it is because I am no painter. I speak of men and things according to my own impressions; who would desire me to speak according to theirs? Let all such write their own books. Though I may be judged as having spoken with undue severity as to some things in the following pages, I hope I have spoken as a Christian; and as an American citizen, who feels that my adopted, beloved country has nothing to learn but evil from the religion, the habits, the morals, the politics, and especially the priests of the Continent of Europe. There are some things which require a whip of scorpions, and they should have it.

I say but little about Ireland, as I indulge the hope of giving a little volume to the public on Ireland and the Irish, for the benefit of its swarming emigrants to this land. But whether I can arrange my materials, and when, are very uncertain—perhaps soon, perhaps never.

I often allude in these pages to my traveling companion. He was Dr. George R. Chetwood, my townsman and friend; eminent for his professional skill and sterling virtues; and who will testify that I have taken no traveler's license with the men, scenes, things, and circumstances which I describe.

I send this volume forth after its predecessor with the prayer to God that all the good seed it contains may be widely scattered and permanently fruitful.

KIRWAN.

New York, August, 1853.

CONTENTS.

CHAPTER XXVIII.

CHAPTER XXIX.

CHAPTER XXX.

CHAPTER XXXI.

CHAPTER XXXII.

CHAPTER XXXIII.

CHAPTER XXXIV.

CHAPTER XXXV.

CHAPTER XXXVI.

CHAPTER XXXVII.

CHAPTER XXXVIII.

CHAPTER XXXIX.

CHAPTER XL.

CHAPTER XLI.

CHAPTER XLII.

CHAPTER XLIII.

CHAPTER XLIV.

MEN AND THINGS

AS SEEN IN EUROPE.

CHAPTER I.

The Voyage opens.—Our Passengers.—A Voyage a Voyage.—A Picture.—Death on Board.—Burial at Sea.—An Ocean Grave undesirable.

THE morning of the 3d of April, 1851, opened brilliantly. A bright blue sky had succeeded to the dripping clouds of the previous day. The fine old packet Montezuma, Captain De Courcey, weighed anchor, and gave her canvas to a favoring northwester. Our sail down the bay of New York, with many friends on board, was as pleasant as could be expected; and when we bid them farewell as they were ordered away, we felt, for the moment, as if some ties were broken that might not again be united. Soon Sandy Hook was passed—soon the Neversink hills died away in the distance, until they seemed as walls propping up the western sky; and when the hour for tea arrived, we could only see the heavens above, and a world of waters around us. We were at sea.

When a man in a crowded hotel is told that he must lodge in the same room with half a dozen of men, the desire instinctively arises to know something of them;

and so, with an imprisonment in the cabin of a ship for a month before you, there is a strong desire to know who are your companions. We met together at the table—we studied each others' physiognomy—and drew our own conclusions. There was the demure, pleasant, intelligent, but dyspeptic physician; the eloquent, learned, but nervous and home-sick divine; the plethoric, gouty, and outspoken Western banker; the thin, tall, sensitive, singular, versatile, imaginative man of letters and fashion, who soon obtained the *soubriquet* of "Professor;" and a short, stout, imperturbable Israelite, with an Abrahamic visage, who soon answered to the name of "Monsieur Gibraltar," and who, from the extent of his travels as a peddler of jewelry, might be taken for the wandering Jew himself. These, with a few others, equally good men but less characteristic, made up our cabin company across the Atlantic.

A voyage is a voyage in all seas and latitudes. All meet with the same incidents. They are sick, and then well. They are now in calm, now in storm. Now they ship a sea, and now they see a ship. And when the passengers have used up all their small talk—and when the medium of pleasant intercourse is all exhausted—and when the weather is cold, and no fire to warm you—and when you are too stupid to write, too cold to read, and too sulky to talk; and when, in addition, you are beset by calms and head winds, I know of nothing more intolerable than a sea voyage. How often did we say that if God would forgive us this time, and return us safe home, we would not be caught committing the sin of going to sea again. But as men soon forget, amid the comforts of wealth, the labor and suffering of its acquisition, so we, amid the new scenes that opened upon us as we traversed the Old World, soon forgot the tedium and suffering of the voyage, and he who complained most is now the most eager to try it again.

One incident, of the deepest interest, occurred during our voyage. There sat on the forward deck, as we went down to the New York bay, a young man with a wan cheek, and pale lips, and sunken eye, which showed that fell consumption was preying upon his vitals. He was a young Irishman returning to his native land in search of health. A female sat by his side—his sister; and when the friends of the passengers were ordered away, they kissed and parted, with the strongest emotions. A widowed mother was expecting him home; and this sister, with throbbing heart, was expecting his return, in improved health. Both were disappointed.

He was a passenger in the second cabin; and as the winds and waves soon placed us all on the sick-list, I lost sight of him for many days, and even his first appearance had passed away from my memory. When our voyage was about half made, a female informed me that a young man in her cabin was very sick, and greatly needed religious instruction. Being informed that a visit from me would be agreeable, I hastened to his berth. My interview with him was deeply affecting. He was a child of Protestant parents. On coming to this country, he had given up all regard for religious things, and lived only for the world and pleasure. A cold had grown into a consumption, which was now near its closing act; and as tenderly as faithfulness would permit, I suggested that, if our voyage should be protracted, as there was reason to fear, he might not live to its close. The thought seemed new and overwhelming, and he turned away and wept. I asked him as to his preparation for eternity. I saw at once, from his answer, the need of a protracted visit; and taking my seat on a greasy trunk by his side, I sought to instruct him into the way of the Lord. I sought in a variety of ways to impress him with a sense of his own sinfulness. I sought to place Christ before him as the only way of escape for sinners—as the only way to heaven; and then, surrounded by his fellow-passengers in the same cabin, I committed him to God in prayer, and especially implored that the ocean might not be made his grave. The effect upon him was not such as I desired; upon others it was deeply solemn.

On the day following he greatly revived, and played cards. The succeeding Sabbath was to be Easter Sunday; and, after the manner of those who regard such times and seasons, he commenced his preparations to keep it. With him and others, it was to be a jolly day. I sent kind inquiries, and asked for another interview; but it was declined *for the present.* On Saturday I learned that he was quite well, and hoped to be on deck on Sunday. There was a change in the weather toward the close of the day. The wind increased the tossing of the ship, and the atmosphere became quite damp. About midnight I was called from my berth to do what I could for the dying man. I crowded my way, half dressed, to his berth, where he lay panting away his life. The glaze of death was already in his eye. The sweat of death was on all his members, His every sense was closed. He was beyond all aid from man. The scene was deeply affecting. There, on the bosom of the wide Atlantic, at midnight, the winds high, and the billows raging, lay a man, surrounded only by strangers, in the last moments of his existence. Nor were these strangers neglectful of him. Women were there, who with maternal and sisterly solicitude ministered to his wants and wept over his sufferings. Feeling that he was beyond my reach, I addressed myself to those around me. The profane swearer, the card-player, the infidel, the Papist were there. But death has power to silence all objections, and to open all ears to serious instruction. I pointed them to the end of all flesh, and to the need of preparation for it; and then implored grace from the God of grace for the dying and the living. I retired to my berth, not to sleep, but to ponder the scene I had just witnessed, the most solemn of my life.

At the dawn of the morning it was announced in my state-room that he was no more. Arrangements were made for his burial after breakfast. At the hour appointed the corpse was brought on deck, sewed up in sail cloth, with a weight attached to its feet. It was laid upon a plank, one end of which extended over the side of the ship, and the other rested on the long boat. The flag of our country, with its stars and stripes, covered the capstan, on which lay a Bible. The passengers and crew were all assembled. There were veteran tars and veteran sinners; but all were affected. There were Protestants and Papists; but all heard with equal interest. I spoke from the text, "And the sea gave up the dead which were in it." And as the great truths pertaining to the resurrection were unfolded, and as the picture was drawn of the wide sea, whose waves seemed to be singing a death dirge around us, giving up all its dead, a solemn stillness pervaded the mixed congregation. The order was now given to bury the corpse; when two sailors gently raised the end of the plank which rested on the long boat, and it slid into its ocean grave. One plunge, and all was over.

While it makes but little differenco where the body is laid, if the spirit is only prepared for its home in the skies, yet there is something greatly undesirable in a burial at sea. Death at sea is usually not expected there. Friends are usually absent. A grave there is away from the sepulchres of our fathers. No mother's tears can bedew it—no stone can mark our resting-place—no hand of affection can plant the cypress, the yew, or the willow at our head; no green grass in the spring, an emblem of the resurrection, will ever cover our narrow house. Our bones may rest as securely among its pearls and corals as on land, but the wide, wild waste above has no attractions. And as the noise of that one plunge sounded through the ship, the silent prayer ascended from my heart to Heaven, "O Lord, if consistent with thy holy will, let none of my descendants to the remotest generation find their grave in the ocean."

CHAPTER II.

First Sight of Land.—Voyage Ended.—Liverpool.—Dr. Raffles.—Souls from Purgatory.—Sabbath in Liverpool.—First Sermon in Britain.—Dr. Hugh M'Neil.—Chat with a Lady.

We were all weary of the sea, and were as anxious for a sight of land as they who watch for the morning.

"Captain," said one of our passengers at dinner, who went by the name of "Colonel of Mooney's brigade," "when shall we see land?"

"About four this afternoon," was the reply. We mustered on deck, and at four the southern coast of Ireland lay dimly in view, and before the day closed rose fully upon us. With what sailors call a "soldier's wind," we beat along the Channel as we could. With the rock-bound shores of Erin in full view, we passed "old head of Kinsale," and afterward the "Tuscar light," and "Holyhead," and the "Skerries," when our gallant ship turned her head toward Liverpool. Soon a pilot was on board; and a "tug" took us in tow; and our sails were furled; and at about ten o'clock on the night of the first of May we turned into one of the Royal Docks for which that city is famed. These docks are easily described. Deep and vast excavations are made on the banks of the Mersey, which are surrounded with solid masonry. These connect with the river by gates, like those which form the locks on our canals. When the tide is full, which rises very high there, these gates are opened, and vessels of any burden pass in and out at pleasure. When the tide commences falling, these gates are closed, and ships of any tonnage ride within them in perfect safety. Such docks require only a high tide and mercantile enterprise to be made any where.

Liverpool is purely a commercial city, displaying little of either taste or beauty. There is much wealth, and solid worth, and active philanthropy there; but its public buildings possess no architectural beauty; its most fashionable residences look plain and dingy; and, with the exception of Prince's Park, which lies outside the city, we observed not a place, or a spot to be compared with any of the parks, or many of the streets which adorn New York or Philadelphia. Save for a man of business, I consider it a most uninviting place of residence.

The name of Dr. Raffles, for many years a distinguished minister of that city, is quite familiar to our American ears. Through a mutual friend, rising to a distinguished rank among the merchants of that city, I had a most pleasant introduction to him. He invited us to breakfast. We went at half past eight, and left at ten o'clock. The visit was remarkably pleasant. He is a man of medium height, of full habit, with a full and fresh English face; his external man strongly recalling to memory the late Dr. Codman, of Dorchester. He is full of information—free and frank in conversation—abounding in anecdote; and these, connected and enlivened with a vein of humor and wit, make him a most agreeable companion. Although probably turned of sixty years, he is yet in the full moon of life, and the active, efficient, beloved pastor of one of the largest congregations of that commercial emporium. With dramatic humor, which exhausted all our power of laughter, he narrated some incidents, illustrating the absurdities of Popery, and the gross frauds practiced by the priests upon their people. Of these the following is a specimen.

An Englishman in Ireland was introduced to a Popish chapel there, when souls were to be delivered from Purgatory. The place was brilliantly lighted. The priest sat at a table on which the relatives of the departed, whose souls were to be released, laid money as they passed. Having collected his wages, the priest commenced his operations, and soon announced that the souls were liberated, and would speedily make their appearance. Immediately a part of the floor opened, and there issued from it small living creatures of red color, to the joyful amazement of all present. One of these creatures jumped near to the Englishman, who seized it, and, putting it in his pocket, rushed out. Breathless, he soon entered the parlor of his friend, exclaiming, as he flung the living creature upon the table, "There is a soul just delivered from Purgatory." It was found to be a frog dressed in red flannel! He was told, as he valued his life, not to reveal the deception, at least until he had crossed the Channel.

While it is difficult to give credence to a story like this, those acquainted with the many uses made of Purgatory to filch money from the pockets of the ignorant and superstitious will not deem it incredible. But it requires the Doctor's manner to give it the effect which it produced upon us. He suited admirably the action to the word, a species of eloquence which can not be printed.

My first sermon in Europe, and the last, was preached in the pulpit of this distinguished minister. I met him, previous to the service, in the vestry, surrounded by his deacons. The sexton was there to put on the gown and bands, which are universally worn by all classes of ministers in Europe. The Bible and hymn book are taken to the pulpit before the preacher enters it. The minister then passes into the church preceded by the sexton, who opens the pulpit door for him and shuts him in. Then the services commence, and are conducted in form and fashion as in our best regulated Presbyterian churches. On this occasion the Doctor conducted the introductory services with a propriety, solemnity, and unction which made them deeply impressive, mingling with his supplications a devout thanksgiving for my happily-ended voyage, and for my merciful deliverance from the perils of the deep. The services ended with the administration of the Lord's Supper, in which I was permitted to unite. I deemed the whole service a merciful beginning and a happy omen of my subsequent Sabbaths and rambles in Europe.

On the evening of the Sabbath, in company with two friends, I went out to hear Dr. Hugh M'Neil, at Prince's Park. He is noted as an eloquent preacher—as an evangelical minister—as a controversialist—a millenarian—and a most bitter Tory politician. It is said that on election eras he preaches politics, as on other occasions he preaches Christ. I was sorry to hear this. His church is large, and cruciform; and in the modern style of Church architecture. A police officer stood at each of its doors to regulate carriages and the goers in. We were ordered by one of these officers from one door to another, and were kept standing in the aisle until service commenced, and might have stood there to its close but for the recognition of my friend by a pew owner. The introductory services were conducted by an assistant or curate; and, when ended, the Doctor entered the pulpit. He is a tall, slender man, straight as an arrow, with grayish hair, and a face of Scotch-Irish cast; for all the world from his neck up like Professor Mulligan of New York. Judging from his face, any body would say that he was predestinated to be a Presbyterian, and of the deepest blue. He was born in Ireland. He took his text from a small Bible which he held in his hand, and which he never laid down during the exercise. His sermon was extempore, calm, expository, truly scriptural, and exceedingly impressive. It contained some passages of great strength, in which he scornfully scouted any definition of the Church which would exclude from it any who truly believe on Christ, and in which he gave to Popery "forty save one." All my feelings were in sympathy with the man and his subject; and I did not wonder that he had been once a competitor for the highest popularity with Irving in London. He was beaten by the Scot.

I could not help saying, at the close of the service, to the lady by whose side I sat, "I hope you feel thankful to God for a minister so truthful and able." "I hope we do, sir," she replied, taking me cordially by the hand. "And who will I tell him was so gratified in hearing him this evening?" she asked. "Will you return him the thanks of a Presbyterian clergyman from America for his excellent sermon, and who spends, to-day, his first Sabbath in England?" was my reply. She again took me by the hand, and with a radiant face replied, "I will go to the vestry and do it instantly." And as I returned from the Church, I could not help wishing that some of our narrow, and selfish, and exclusive ministers of the High-Church cut, in our own free country, could have heard Dr. M'Neil with me on that occasion. The Low-Church ministers of England are far more outspoken than in this country. Not merely Oxfordism, but the exclusive dogmas of High-Churchism, which give over other Christians to uncovenanted mercies, they denounce in words that burn. They are not dependent, as here, upon the bishops, for their places and stipends. There is no pecuniary motive to silence. Never will I forget the lashing which the noble stammering Bishop Daly gave them—of which more anon.

Thus was spent my first Sabbath in England.

CHAPTER III.

Ride from Liverpool to London.—Chat in the Cars.—London.—Samuel Gurney.—Reform in Ireland.—Rev. Mr. Jowett.—John Henderson.—Dr. Achilli.—Caution as to Priests.

The Station-house at Liverpool is quite an affair, and is managed with a quietness and promptness which surprises those who only know the bustle, noise, and rudeness of railway depôts and officials in America. The railway cars are divided into three apartments, each containing six persons. With the assistance of an English lady, well-bred and intelligent, and somewhat beyond the medium dimensions, there were enough of us from America to fill one of the departments. We were off at the appointed moment—we were soon lost in the darkness of the tunnel through which you leave the city—and after you emerge again into the light, the villas, the cultivation, the green swards, the beautiful hedge-rows of Old England opened upon our view. Soon we commenced our comparisons of things in our own country with those which every where attracted our attention, and the truth of the old adage, "comparisons are odious," was soon apparent in the conduct of our English friend. With noble heroism, she advanced to the defense of "her own, her native land." We admired her cleverness and shrewdness, while we could not help a smile occasionally at her ignorance of our country. We had many a pass, as pleasant as they were mirthful, which made us forget that we were flying toward London at the rate of nearly fifty miles an hour. At length, when pushed a little harder than politeness toward a lady would warrant from Americans, she sought to silence us all by the magnificent sentence, "but all that man, wealth, cultivation, and taste can do, they have done for England."

"True, madam," was the reply; "but all that God can do he has done for our country. Man has made England, but God has made America."

"I give up, I give up," she replied, with a hearty laugh. Soon we reached London, and separated, feeling that some, at least, of the spice of life consists in variety of opinion, and not esteeming each other the less because of it. The blunt honesty of the English, even when it approaches rudeness, as it often does, in the advocacy of what they esteem right, is much more to my taste than the gum-elastic pliancy of the French, who sacrifice every thing to politeness.

We are now in London, the world's Babel, and its greatest centre of influence. It is so well known, and is so much like some of the older parts of some of our older cities, that I shall not undertake to describe it. After taking rooms at Woods', High Holborn, and arranging our money affairs for the Continent, we went out to do duty and to see sights. My first call was upon Samuel Gurney, the brother of the well known John I. Gurney, and of Mrs. Fry, to whom I had a note of introduction from the late Dr. Griscom, of scientific and philanthropic memory. He is a plain Quaker, wearing the full dress of his people, of strong physical development, and of a pleasing benignant aspect.

He is at the head of a large banking house, and his time and fortune are freely devoted to all efforts to do good. He well sustains the reputation of a family which has an American as well as a European reputation for well doing. He offered me the hospitalities of his house, and to introduce me to some of the benevolent institutions of the city, which my other arrangements compelled me to decline. He stated, among other efforts to do good, one in which he and some of his friends were engaged in reference to Ireland, which consisted in buying large tracts of land, sold under a recent act of Parliament, and then reselling them in small farms, in fee simple, to the farmers of the country. This plan, if made universal, would soon work the redemption and elevation of that unhappy island.

Thence I went to the rooms of the British and Foreign Bible Society, which was to hold its anniversary on the following day, and delivered my credentials as a delegate from its sister society in America, and was most kindly and cordially received by its secretaries. I there met the venerable Mr. Jowett, brother of the famed missionary in the East. He is a man of middle size, gray, and perfectly blind. He was led about by a young girl. After a brief conversation, in which he showed a heart intensely alive to the cause of Christ, I rose to take my departure, saying, "We shall soon be where we can both speak to and *see* one another." He instantly replied, with a warm pressure of the hand, "We shall see Christ as he is, which is far better." I was deeply affected by the sight of the apostolical man, laid aside, in Providence, from his labors, led about by the hand of a maid, with sightless eye-balls seeking light and finding none. How joyful must be the anticipations of Heaven to such a saint, just putting off his harness!

At a meeting for prayer, held morning and evening at our hotel, I was introduced to John Henderson, Esq., of Park, one of the princely merchants of Glasgow, who came up to London to preside at the meeting of the Tract Society. He is a well-known friend of the religious press, was the chief agent in getting up and getting out the prize essays on the Sabbath, one of which is entitled "The Pearl of Days," and also a most valuable volume, which has not been reprinted in this country, entitled "The Christian Sabbath," and which consists of a series of sermons by some of the ablest clergymen of North and South Britain. From this gentleman and Christian, from whom I received many acts of kindness both in London and Scotland, I received an invitation to breakfast at his rooms, in company with the far-famed Dr. Achilli. Greatly desirous of an interview with this reformed priest, I accepted the invitation.

We met at eight at the rooms of Mr. Henderson, and separated at ten. Dr. Achilli, an Italian by birth, a Papist and priest by education, and subsequently a popular preacher and professor, is now, as the world knows, a Protestant. His imprisonment in the Inquisition, his escape thence, the charges preferred against him by Father Newman and Cardinal Wiseman, and the developments made in the recent trial of Newman for slander, have given him great notoriety. He is a short man, firmly built, with jet black hair, and a black and restless eye. His age may be an advance on forty years. His manners are pleasant, and in conversation he is free—decidedly talkative. Although his English was very broken, and my Italian in a far worse condition, we needed no interpreter. Beyond all men that I ever heard, he was dead upon Popery and the priests. His competency as a witness none can question. And, until I saw Naples and Rome for myself, I supposed his fierce persecution by his former friends gave a tinge of bitterness to his testimony. Now I can believe any thing as to the shameless immoralities and gross corruption of the Italian priests. He said he was engaged in a translation of the New Testament into Italian for the Baptist Bible Society of New York. We had quite a discussion as to the meaning of the word "baptize," in which he showed but little acquaintance with the history of the controversy or with the Greek, and in which he admitted the validity of baptism by water, in any quantity, while he betrayed a preference to the mode by immersion.

I am free to confess that I was not so favorably impressed as I expected to have been. It is hard thoroughly to purge a man from the virus of Popery, who has practiced for years together the wicked jugglery of its priesthood. God can do it; but, as a rule, we should wait for good evidence that it is done. The barrel, emptied of a bitter liquid, long retains its scent and its taste. I have read the Newman trial with some care; and while it pours confusion upon Rome and her priests, I confess I should not wonder if there were some grounds for the charges against Achilli. What reason have we to suppose that, while a priest in Italy, he did not live as do Italian priests? But since his hopeful conversion, every effort and witness failed to prove moral delinquency. May he endure to the end and be saved.

As light and truth are extending, Papal priests are surrendering their wicked and deceptive trade, and the number of such must increase from year to year. But Protestant churches should know that conversion *from* Popery is not conversion *to* Christ. And we should wait for more than ordinary evidence as to the conversion of a man who spent years in converting a wafer into God, in hearing confessions and forgiving sins for fifty cents a head, in massing souls out of Purgatory, and in deceiving ignorant people by other priestly fabrications, before we admit him to the privileges and immunities of the Christian Church. It takes time thoroughly to imbue a mind with the spiritualism of Christianity which has long been accustomed to regard it as a matter of ceremony.

CHAPTER IV.

Exeter Hall.—Meeting of the British and Foreign Bible Society.—Lord Ashley.—Marquis of Cholmondeley.—Earl of Harrowby.—Sir Robert H. Ingles.—Dr. Duff.—Salt among the Aristocracy.

THE meeting of the British and Foreign Bible Society is the great anniversary of London. The great rally of Protestantism is on its platform. There, all who receive the Bible as the all-sufficient Rule of Faith—forgetting all minor differences—meet, and rejoice together in the privileges and blessings of our common Christianity. Accompanied by a few friends, we went early to the Committee-room at Exeter Hall, where we were introduced to the officers of the society, the speakers, and to the noblemen, gentlemen, and clergymen, who were present in considerable number. At the appointed hour we entered, by a side door, the platform of the hall itself, headed by Lord Ashley, the president, and were received with applause by the crowd of spectators. This famous hall is a large oblong room, without galleries, with an elevated platform at one end, and the seats rising toward the other. It reminds an American, not so much of the Tabernacle at New York, as of the Musical Fund Hall of Philadelphia. Being the representative of our American Bible Society, I was assigned a prominent seat, next but one to the President; and, although surrounded by the nobles of the land and the dignitaries of the Church, they were as plain and as unpretending men in their appearance as we ever meet in good society. In point of pretension, a New York clerk or Puseyite priest would beat any of them.

After the reading of a portion of Scripture, Lord Ashley, who then presided for the first time as president, rose, and uttered a brief but noble speech. It was full of sense, piety, and noble Protestantism. And when he uttered the sentence, "the evangelization of the nations and the peace of the world depend upon the full, free, and universal circulation of the Word of God," a plaudit rose from the vast assembly, loud and long, which it was good to hear. This nobleman, now the Earl of Shaftsbury, is making his mark upon his age. He is at the head of the Ragged School system, if not its originator. He is devoting his fortune, the influence of his position, and his personal industry, to the instruction and elevation of the lowest classes of society. He is yet in mid-life, tall, spare, of light complexion, easy, kind, and modest in manner, and bearing a most striking resemblance to the lamented Dr. Kearney Rodgers, of New York. "May he live," in the language of the Celestials, "a thousand years."

There sat down by my side a small man shortly after the meeting opened, who was greeted with some "ruffling" as he entered by the side door. During the reading of the report, he was making marks on the floor with a small ratan. "The first resolution will be offered by the Marquis of Cholmondeley," said the President, when, to my no little amazement, up jumped my left-hand neighbor, offered the resolution, and made quite a speech. I had no idea I was so near a marquis, and while I saw in his address but little thought or force, the audience must have seen it full of both, as they clapped him most profusely. But I soon saw that the clapping always rose or fell with the title of the speaker. We had a similar speech from the Earl of Harrowby, which for its fulsome eulogy of the new president was intolerable, and whose redeeming quality was a vein of earnest piety.

The name of Sir Robert H. Ingles, then member of Parliament for Oxford, was announced. He is a man of mark in the House, and his connection with Romanizing Oxford excited some interest. He has rendered himself quite famous recently by his awful review of the Bishop of Exeter, in which he leaves neither root nor branch of that vain, turbulent, selfish, but very clever prelate, who once honestly wrote a powerful pamphlet against Catholic emancipation, and then answered it for a mitre; and who exercises his apostolical functions and patronage so discreetly as to pension almost all his poor relations with fat offices. The speech of the noble baronet was truly excellent; and a feeling of deep solemnity pervaded the entire auditory when he said with emotion and self-application, "No man ought to stand up here to advocate the diffusion of the Bible, unless he makes it his first duty to regulate his own life and heart by its precepts. Whether we have placed the Bible or not in the hands of the negro, the Esquimaux, or the Chinese, matters little to any of us personally, unless we have the Bible in our own hearts." Sir Robert is a large, portly man, with a full, rosy face, fluent utterance, decidedly and subjectively pious, and was, on the whole the most perfect personification of an Englishman on the platform. Unless he relishes his roast beef, his plum pudding, and his mug of ale, he should have his outer man indicted for bearing false testimony against him.

The Bishop of Cashel was announced from the chair, and my right-hand neighbor was on his feet in a moment. He seemed eager for the opportunity. He is a strongly built, frank, stammering Irishman, with clearly defined principles and strong emotions. And how fearfully he lashed High-Churchism and Oxfordism! Much as I dislike both of them, I felt like asking my brother bishop to have a little mercy. "Nothing," he said, "promotes Roman Catholicism like departing in any thing from the Scriptures. If the simple Scriptures had been adhered to in certain portions of our Church, we should never have heard, first, of the semi-popery, and then of the whole popery of those who have left a stain upon the Church which they have deserted. Long before people knew they had a tinge of Popery, they were too High-Church to be members of the Bible Society. They have deserted the Church of England, but they have not deserted the Bible Society, for they never belonged to it." Would that those in our country, in and out of the Episcopal denomination, who are for treating High-Churchism in its modern developments gingerly, could have heard the lashing given it by the Lord Bishop of Cashel, in Exeter Hall. It would have nerved their energies to treat its assumptions as they richly deserve. Bad, in many respects, as is the Irish establishment, it has too much of Popery around it to fall in love with any of its tricks or devices. There is no Puseyism in Ireland. There should be none within the wide domain of Protestantism.

But, beyond all question, the man of the meeting was Dr. Duff, the great Scotch missionary at Calcutta. I had heard of him—I had read his powerful and moving addresses and communications, but now I saw and heard him. The day was chilly, and he sat near me, wrapped up in a cloak. He is quite tall, probably six feet two or three inches, when he takes the folds out of his body. He is a very slender man, with a small head, thick black hair, combed back from his forehead and temples, deep-sunken black eyes, hollow cheeks, and presenting, on the whole, a worn, sickly aspect. His accent is of the broadest Scotch, and his delivery most furious. When his name was announced, the hall rang again. He commenced like a race-horse, and kept in full gallop to the close of a very long speech. He twisted his body into all possible shapes—at one time, a part of the tail of his coat was over his shoulder; at another, he had every available portion of it closely packed under one arm, so as to reveal his waistcoat midway to his shoulders. I never heard such a torrent of information, of history, of invective, of figure and illustration, of vigorous grappling with pantheism, infidelity, and formalism, and of earnest exhortation to the whole host of God's elect to a bold and united assault upon the army of the aliens. And as he traced the progress of the soul emerging from the darkness of nature into the light of revelation, and by the aid of that light ascending step by step until introduced to the general assembly and Church of the First-born in heaven, he held his audience in breathless silence.

When he concluded his speech he was dripping with perspiration; and the moment his last words were uttered, he rolled his cloak around him, and, amid the tumultuous applause of the house, darted out of the hall.

This meeting of the British and Foreign Bible Society had other besides religious interest to me. There were seen to meet and mingle all classes of men and Christians on the common platform of their humanity and Christianity. Dukes and earls were there in common dress, plain as the plainest; and if there was any difference, with less force of intellect than their untitled brethren. Yet it was charming to see their position and influence on the right side, and to hear the strain of humble, fervent, earnest piety that ran through all their speeches. There is much salt mingled with the corruption which pervades the English aristocracy. Lord Ashley, Sir Robert Ingles, and the Earl of Harrowby, are not, however, true samples of their class. They form the exceptions.

CHAPTER V.

St. Paul's.—The Tower.—The Thames.—Westminster Abbey.—Stone of Destiny.—Regent's Square Church.—Dr. Hamilton.—St. James's.—Westminster.—Bishop Wilberforce.

The Cathedral of Saint Paul's, London, is a huge superstructure, surmounting a hill, in a crowded part of the city, near the Thames. Its immense walls are being covered with the memorials of great men, who by sea and land have extended and are extending the dominion of England. It did not impress us as we expected, and we felt that the busts and boasting epitaphs of naval and military commanders might be somewhere else than in a house consecrated to the worship of God.

The Tower of London is a collection of many buildings inclosed within a wall, whose gates are strongly guarded. Its bloody history is known in all the earth. We were shown the Armory, a long room crowded with men on horseback, illustrating the kind of armor worn for six centuries past. The waiter, in harlequin dress, who conducts you through it, gives you a brief and rapid history of each knight, and gets you on and out as quickly as possible. He gives you not a minute to sketch, note, or consider. The small, secluded room, where are deposited the crown and crown jewels, is an object of curiosity. Our company was counted as we entered it; we were then given over to quite a dainty old lady in cap and gloves, who took us around a glass case, and gave us a hurried account of the various articles it inclosed, which she valued at twenty millions, but whether pounds or dollars I do not remember, nor is it material. We were again counted as we went out, and the door was shut. To one whose heart has often bled in reading of the atrocities there committed, and whose imagination has magnified it into a most massive and towering prison, a frowning relic of barbarism, it is a most flat affair. Its bloody history alone invests it with the least interest, and there are but few bloodier spots in Europe. As you pass over its rough pavements and through its dark passages, you feel as if haunted by the ghosts of the queens, princes, nobles, saints, and sinners who were there legally and illegally murdered. What a bloody history is that of England!

A sail up or down the Thames is a curious affair. It runs through the city, and is one of the great thoroughfares of the town. It is crowded with small steamers, which stop at given points for receiving and discharging passengers, which is done with great rapidity. It was our lot to see it and sail upon it when the tide was down, and then the stream was small, the current rapid, and the bed of the river exceedingly filthy. Above the London Bridge, the rear of the houses and warehouses run down to the river, which renders the prospect any thing but pleasant to those upon its waters. Paris has made every thing of the Seine, and Dublin much of the Liffy, but London has made nothing of the Thames for its adornment. Its shipping and great docks lie below the London Bridge.

Westminster Abbey is a fine specimen of the old

Gothic architecture. Days might be spent in viewing and noting its points of interest, and the tombs of the illustrious in letters. Its general plan is that of a Latin cross. In the Poet's Corner are the monuments of the most distinguished poets of England; in other parts of it are those of statesmen, warriors, scholars, and artists, who have shed lustre on the British name. The monarchs of England are crowned in its choir, where under the coronation chair is the famous stone "Lia fail," or "stone of destiny," on which the kings of Ireland were crowned for ages, and which had the peculiar property of giving forth a terrific sound when any of the royal Scythian race was crowned upon it, and of being silent on all other occasions. It was taken from Tara to Scone, in Scotland, and thence to England, and over it the coronation chair now stands. The star of empire is said to be governed by the movements of this stone! The Irish legends have much to say about the "Lia fail," and the good genius of Ireland yet weeps over its removal. With its return to Tara there will be a return of empire!

I declined all invitations to preach in London, that I might spend a Sabbath in hearing and seeing for myself. As a good Presbyterian, I went to the church on Regent Square, to hear the Rev. Dr. Hamilton, so favorably known in our own country by several attractive, popular, and truly evangelical works. This is the church in which Irving once preached with a popularity which has never been equaled—when prime ministers, dukes, and nobles were willing to enter by a window to hear him. The church is plain, but substantial and large. I entered it before service commenced, and was shown to a backless bench in the middle aisle! I had the consolation of seeing others, male and female, treated with equal politeness. After the service commenced we were invited to empty pews, of which there were several. Others accepted, but I declined the honor; and, partly out of ill humor with their way of treating strangers, I kept my backless seat through the service. Instead of Dr. Hamilton, my old friend Dr. Cunningham, so widely and favorably known in America, rose in the pulpit and performed the entire service. It was a missionary sermon from 2 Cor., v., 14, 15—full of matter, sound, long, and exhaustive of the text. It was Scotch throughout. After service I was introduced, in the vestry, to Dr. Hamilton, with whom I went to dinner, in company with Dr. Cunningham. Dr. Hamilton is very like his books—pleasant, imaginative, free in conversation, full of information, cheerful, with face, accent, and manner which would prove his north Tweed origin if met in the moon.

Hearing that Wilberforce, bishop of Oxford, was to preach a charity sermon in St. James's, Westminster, in company with Dr. Cunningham, I took a very long walk to hear him. The house was thronged when we reached it, and we went into the gallery. I took a stand in front of a seat which had two persons in it, but there was no invitation to enter. After keeping my standing position for some time, I heard my name rather audibly whispered into the ear of the beef-headed John Bull that kept the seat, and by some person who had seen me at Exeter Hall, when I was invited in. My temper was much the same as at Regent's Square; but, as my feet were not in the best condition to sustain it,

I bowed and entered. The service was read intolerably, and was rendered ludicrous in one portion of it, where the minister paused, and, by way of parenthesis, gave the name of a lady who desired to offer public thanks for her safe delivery of a son! The singing was performed by boys. The Bishop was heralded from the vestry by a man wearing a military chapeau, and holding in his hand a wand of office; he conducted him to the pulpit, arranged his robes, and shut him in. His text was John, xvi., 26, and the sermon was decidedly the poorest I heard in Europe. It was short, pointless, and, save in a single paragraph at the close, without any reference to the subject for which the collection was solicited. He is said to be one of the ablest bishops on the bench, and if his was a specimen of their preaching, I could most devoutly unite in the language of the Liturgy, and pray, from such homilies, "may the good Lord deliver us." The Bishop is a short, not handsome man, of youthful appearance, with considerable character for cleverness and eloquence. He is regarded as a Tractarian, and as sympathizing in many things with some of his kindred who have already gone to Rome. He so manages, however, as to excite the hopes and the fears of each of the parties into which the Church of England is divided, each party having claimed and disowned him. To such an extent has he carried this double dealing, as to have secured for himself the appellation of "Slippery Sam."

How must the sainted spirit of William Wilberforce regard, from its abode on high, the unworthy conduct of his erring sons! Well said Solomon, that we know not who shall come after us, whether they be wise men or whether they be fools.

CHAPTER VI.

Mr. Lawrence.—Parliament House.—House of Lords.—Lord Chancellor. — Duke of Argyle. — Wee Willie Skinner. — Lord Grey. — Bishop Wilberforce.—Tout ensemble.—Law Lords.—Sir Culling Eardley.—Badinage.

THROUGH the kindness of Mr. Lawrence, our minister at the Court of St. James, and who, by his urbanity, ability, and attentions to his countrymen, has won for himself golden opinions in all quarters, myself and traveling companion got admission to the House of Lords. This is an apartment in the new House of Parliament, just as our Senate Chamber is an apartment in the Capitol at Washington. By-the-way, the Parliament House, now approaching completion, struck me as greatly un-English. It looks unsubstantial and undignified, because of the profusion of its ornamental and filagree work. It impresses you as does a very large lady with manifold pretensions, flounced and ruffled from head to foot. When finished, it will be, however, a great affair. It stands on the Thames and opposite to Westminster Abbey, the street only separating them.

The way to the gallery of the House of Lords is just about as plain as is the way to the gallery of our own House of Representatives, or Senate Chamber, in Washington. You need either a guide, or to be taught to thread the labyrinth. We were shown the way, and entered the gorgeous apartment. It is an oblong room, most richly carved and gilded, with the throne on one end, and the gallery in which we sat on the other. The doors of admission to the floor were on either side of the throne and opposite to us; there must have been one or more beneath us, as on the adjournment the Lord Chancellor made his exit in that direction. The "Woolsack" is a plain, oblong settee, without back, placed in the middle of the room, and upon which the Lord Chancellor sat, who seems to act as the presiding officer of the body, although never so addressed. Each speaker addresses "My Lords." The members sit upon plain benches, rising like steps one above another. The furnishing, and the carving, and gilding of the room form a very strong contrast. We were seated by an English clergyman who was acquainted with the persons of all the peers, and who was ready to answer all our questions. The woolsack was occupied by the Chancellor in his robes, and buried in an enormous wig of office. My friend asked me if he did not remind me of quite an old lady in my congregation, now verging toward eighty years! The Duke of Argyle was there, tall, straight, bold, with hair as red as a lobster, and, from what I saw, of corresponding temper. He is the man who, having partaken of the communion in the Episcopal Chapel in Glasgow, with his wife, was afterward excommunicated for partaking of it in his own church, the Presbyterian. The Bishop who issued the bull is a small, crooked man, formed after the pattern of a note of interrogation. The bull commenced thus: "We, William Skinner, Bishop," &c.; and from that day to this, he is laughed at all over Britain as "Wee Willy Skinner." Lord Stanley was there, now ex-prime minister, tall, thin, thoughtful, buttoned up to his chin, and apparently in poor health. Lord Grey was there, son of a former premier, of most ungainly aspect, his knees boxing when he walked, as if bending under the weight of his slender form. There was quite a mixture of the fat and the lean, the tall and the short, the smart and the stupid. There was the Bishop of Cork, in full canonicals, old and infirm.

"And who is that?" said I to my neighbor, as a lord spiritual entered, dressed in lawn, and took his seat.

"Wilberforce, bishop of Oxford," was the reply; "and one of the most able and eloquent debaters here."

"I heard him preach a wretched sermon yesterday, at St. James's," said I.

"Oh, he does not care much about preaching; he lays out his strength here," said my kind informant.

"What kind of a man is he?" I asked.

"Well, I do not know; we all call him 'Slippery Sam,'" was the reply.

"And who is that?" said I, as a fine person entered, rotund, bald, affable in manner, and of pleasant and mild aspect.

"The richest peer of England, the Marquis of Westminster," was the reply.

The stars of the House were not there—the Iron Duke had just rode away from the House as we approached it.

On the whole, I was most unfavorably impressed with all I saw in the Upper House. All wore their hats save when they rose to speak; then they took them off, and put them on again as soon as they ended. They walked about without any restraint. The old men looked stupid—indeed, one was asleep—and the young lords, who formed the majority, seemed trifling in their manners and appearance. I know not of a point in which they do not fail in comparison with the Senate of the United States, especially when adorned by Clay, Webster, and Calhoun. And the question arises, Why do the decisions of such a body upon great law points carry such weight over that empire upon which the sun never sets? The reason is, that the "Law Lords" alone decide such points. In theory every Lord has a vote, but the carrying out of the theory would be contrary to that uniform practice which has given symmetry, and uniformity, and confidence to the judicial decisions of the House of Lords. Is there not a lesson here for our country to learn?

The name of Sir Culling Eardley is known to the extreme boundaries of philanthropy and religion. I was introduced to him by Mr. Henderson, of Park, and accepted an invitation to spend an evening at his beautiful residence at Belvidere, about fourteen miles from London, on the Thames. He is a man of middle size, pleasant, affable, well educated, simple in his manners, and a zealous, humble Christian. The evening I spent in his family, in company with a gentleman from India and a minister from France, will not be soon forgotten.

"To what Church do you belong, sir?" said Lady Eardley to me, as I sat by her side at the tea-table.

"To the Presbyterian," was my reply.

"Dear me!" said she; "from the way in which Sir Culling spoke of you, I supposed you were an American bishop."

"Well, I am," I replied.

The following conversation then arose, to the no little amusement of Sir Culling and his friend from India, both of whom had seceded from the Episcopal

Church, while Lady Eardley has continued her adherence to it.

"Do you Presbyterians believe in bishops ?"

"Certainly ; as all our standards teach."

"And how do you ordain ministers ?"

"By the laying on of the hands of the bishops composing a Presbytery."

"In what, then, do you Presbyterians differ from us Episcopalians ?"

"In this : we have more bishops than you, and more dioceses. We make every minister settled over a parish a bishop, and we make every parish a diocese. And if you would do so here in England, you would have far less trouble than you do."

"Well, I have never understood the difference between you and us before ; and I do not know but that it would be a great improvement upon our Church to introduce your system into England. What do you think, Sir Culling ?"

While he made no reply, laughing merrily at the badinage, I have no doubt but that he heartily assented to the improvement it would make in England to convert every parish into a diocese, and every good minister into a bishop. It would certainly save them from such flares-up as the Philpotts of Exeter make. Generations to come will call Sir Culling blessed. In many of his expectations from his Alliance I deem him visionary. Yet he will have his reward. He has the heart of a philanthropist. The glory of England would be resplendent as the sun if all its aristocracy were like him. He is unwearied in well-doing, and in due time he will reap his reward.

CHAPTER VII.

London to Dover.—Dover.—A Voyage to Calais.—Official Imposition.—Landing in France.—A true Picture.—Ride from Calais to Paris.—The Country.—Wind-mills.—People.—A Dissertation on Vanes.

The railway from London to Dover lies through a beautiful though level country. To an American accustomed to the bold scenery of the Hudson, and who has crossed the Alleghanies, and who has spent years among the Green Mountains, England seems quite tame in physical aspect; to a traveler from Switzerland, it seems level as the ocean in a calm. In the month of May, a magnificent cultivation every where presents itself. Dover is a very bleak place, lying under snowy chalk cliffs upon the sea. All the surrounding hills are covered with the strongest fortifications, which in the distance look like old ruins, that add so much to the romantic beauty of the Rhine. They look out upon the old enemy of England, and are kept in the finest repair. Upon one of their walls lay for a long time the famous old cannon, pointing over the Channel, upon whose breech was written the sentence,

> "Keep me dry, and keep me clean,
> And I'll carry a ball to Calais green."

The town itself looks like a poor old man of eighty years, all whose friends had preceded him to the tomb. As the rail-car turns the point where you get your first sight of the Channel, the shores of France lie in full view.

We were here hurried on board a miserable steamer for Calais, built after the very worst fashion of these vessels in England. It was dignified by some royal name, and belonged to some royal company, and was commanded by some captain of her majesty's royal service! Who ever heard of royal names so contemptibly bestowed! The wind was fresh, and the sea rough. As soon as we left the shelter of the pier, we were all drenched by the spray of the short, chopping waves dashing our bark, and from which there was no possible protection. Soon all were sick. My worst Atlantic sickness was drinking nectar in comparison to this! And before we were half seas over, and while yet sweating under the violence of our ejections, a man with a gold band around his cap stood before me, and demanded, in true John Bull accent, "Your ticket." I had paid in London through to Paris; I handed him my ticket. "Four shillings, sir," said he. "For what?" said I. "For your seat in the boat, and for attendance," he replied. "I have paid to Paris, and I have had no attendance," I answered. "Four shillings—you might have had attendance if you asked for it," he bluffly replied. As well as a person almost sick unto death could do it, I found, slowly, four shillings, and as I slowly counted them into his hands, I said to him, "You and your government should be indicted, first, for such wretched accommodations upon such a thoroughfare; and, next, for your gross impositions." I think I was less amiable between Dover and Calais than I remember to have been during any part of my journey. If her majesty's servant was not cut by what I said, it was not my fault. I put on my sentence the keenest edge I could; but such officials have usually a very hard skin. Theirs is the scaly hide of the leviathan. If such extortions were practiced in the United States, they would be bruited through Europe as Americanisms.

Until I placed my foot on the quay of Calais, I maintained a home feeling, but when I saw men of foreign aspect all around me, and heard them shouting in a foreign tongue, the feeling fled. I was in a strange land! My little French was put immediately into requisition; but the vacant stare, and the "non comprendre" of the Frank soon made me feel that my accent, or idiom, or both, were at fault. And I returned the compliment of "non comprendre," when a Frenchman, wishing to do me a service "for a compensation," poured a torrent of French into my face. On hearing a Frenchman speak, it has always seemed to me as if his words were all connected, without space, comma, colon, or period to divide them, as if they came out in a continuous stream, just like a jet of water. But never did this seem so to me to the same degree as at Calais, when surrounded by porters, waiters, commissionaires, each anxious to secure the privilege of waiting on you, and on as many others as possible. To have half a dozen of men bowing to you—talking to you—wishing to serve you—recommending a hotel here—a restaurant there—one asking for your passport—another ready to fly off with your baggage, and not to understand a word they say, and only able to conjecture what they wish to do; and then to be at your wits' ends to know where to turn, and ready to die with laughter at the efforts all around you of the English to speak French, and of the French to speak English—if this is not a picture of an American landing from a crazy English steamer, the remembrance of which makes him sea-sick, on the quay at Calais, then my readers may draw their own picture, and to their own liking. However others felt on that memorable day, I felt that I was from home!

Calais, which I care not to see again until Victoria provides a better steamer, until I speak French, or the people learn English, is a walled town, and strongly fortified. It looks out upon Dover with jealous eye, and was for two centuries the key of the British possessions in France. There we took the cars, and after slowly winding out of the town, we hastened on our way through Lille, Douay, Arras, Amiens, and Clermont, to Paris. The country is level through the whole route, with scarcely a hillock to break the dull monotony. Arras, the birth-place of the bloody Robespierre, lives by wind-mills. As the rail-car made a rapid semicircle round the city, I strove to count them, but such was the confusion made by the tossing of their huge arms in the air, I soon gave it up as hopeless. The lands are well cultivated, and some places of great beauty occasionally present themselves to the eye; but the people of the country seem every where in the raw material. Every where the women were seen working in the fields, and in one case we saw a man and woman drawing a harrow. Papal churches were very numerous, but their steeples were surmounted by roosters instead of crosses. Why a rooster? I would request a certain ecclesiological society, formed some time since in New-York, to direct their profound investigations to the solution of this question. Bats, owls, and roosters, I should think, were very much in their line. There is some difference between crosses and roosters, and as the latter may have some reference to the cock whose crowing brought Peter to repentance, it is a matter of grave inquiry which should surmount a steeple. In this day of emblems there ought to be an effort at uniformity upon this matter. Some steeples are surmounted by weather-vanes —some by crosses—some by balls—and, sad to narrate, one, at least, by a pumpkin! but I am free to confess, that if they could only crow, and if their crowing would only have the effect of one of old upon those who trace their ecclesiastical descent from Peter or Judas, I would vote for roosters. Besides, a rooster is a most portly bird, and walks with a proud tread, and a high head, and quite an air of authority among his barn-yard family; and what better emblem does the world afford of a modern successor of the apostles? I go for chanticleer versus crosses. I like his archiepiscopal air!

We left London after breakfast in the morning, and took tea at Paris in the evening, flying from city to city in twelve hours! Before nine in the evening we were resting in our rooms in the Hotel Windsor, in Rue Rivoli, which looks out upon the magnificent garden of the Tuileries.

CHAPTER VIII.

Paris.—Garden or the Tuileries: its Beauty.—Night Walk.—Palais Royal: its Gardens.—Arbre de Cracovie.—Jardin des Plantes.—Père la Chaise: its Epitaphs.

PARIS! Paris! of world-wide fame for its splendor, its palaces, its fashions, its arts, its revolutions, its wickedness, its rivers of blood, its cooks, and its milliners—I am now in Paris! As it has no environs like London, you pass at once from an open country into a crowded city. And as you are driven from the depôt, through narrow streets, to your hotel, you are overwhelmed with disappointment, and ask at every turn, is this Paris? Many of its most fashionable streets are as narrow as Nassau Street, in New York; are without any side walks, paved with round stones, and with a channel in the centre to carry off the water! In treading your way through them, you have to dodge the wagons, carriages, and people as you can. And yet Paris is a magnificent city; but its beauty lies in spots. I will describe things as I saw them.

After a pleasant night's rest, a little farther from the earth than would be convenient in case of fire or earthquake, myself and friend sallied out to see sights. Our first walk was through the garden of the Tuileries from the palace, through the Place de la Concorde, Champs Elysées, up, up to the triumphal arch, L'Etoile. Frenchmen say that this is the most beautiful promenade in the world. And I have no reason to question it. Starting from the main entrance of the famous old Palace, whose every window and chamber have their bloody history, and walking leisurely along through shady groves, by magnificent fountains, greeted at every turn by the finest chiseled statuary—with the Madeleine, and the Palace of Ministers on the one hand, with the Hotel d'Orsay, the Palais Bourbon, and the Chamber of Deputies on the other, from which you are separated by the Seine with its graceful bridges, your emotions of pleasure increase at every step, until you are overwhelmed. You can do little more than stand, gaze, and wonder. And beautiful as is this walk by day, it is still more enchanting by night; when, with the stars overhead, and every avenue and fountain brilliantly lighted, and marble men and women gazing upon you from every mound and from under every tree, and with the soothing notes of music floating around you wherever you wander over the vast area of beauty and magnificence, you feel the magic effect melting you into sympathy with the scenes around you. I doubt whether the world can present any thing to be compared in beauty to that portion of Paris which lies between the Palace of the Tuileries and the Triumphal Arch, that noble monument to the memory of Napoleon the Great.

The Palais Royal is another of the beautiful spots of Paris. It is said to be to Paris what Paris is to France. It covers an entire square, built up on all sides, with splendid entrances to the enchanting grounds that form the centre. This palace, with its gardens, courts, galleries, and arcades, is the great central point of pleasure.

C

In this garden was the celebrated tree—the famous "arbre de Cracovie"—under whose shade politicians decided the fate of nations. Every thing here is intended for the gratification of the senses. There is nothing here pure, natural, spiritual—and the uncorrupted stranger soon wishes himself away from the intoxicating labyrinth. Here are restaurants, gambling-rooms, wine, milliner, and jewelry shops on the most gorgeous scale. In these gardens may be found, early in the morning, the tradesmen—at nine, the coffee-houses begin to fill—from twelve to two, the gay world is there—from two to five, the avenues are crowded with nursery-maids and children—about eight, the women of the town make their appearance, when every thing is brilliantly illuminated, and every thing is bustle, gay, noisy, and intoxicating until twelve, when the crowd melts away. The Palais Royal presents, on a fine night, a true picture of the frivolity, luxury, versatility, sensuality, and corruption of the French people. It is a brilliant spot, and there are but few in the world where more sin is committed in each twenty-four hours in the year. It is said to be changing for the better.

The Jardin des Plantes forms another of the great attractions of this great city. Here the taste and science of Buffon and Cuvier are remarkably displayed. Its botanic gardens are extensive and most elegantly arranged. Its cabinets of minerals are on the largest scale. Its zoological gardens contain every animal under heaven. . And here are delivered lectures on the natural sciences, by the most eminent savans, at public expense, and to about 1800 students, from April to October in each year. This Jardin is the pride of France, and has been alike regarded by Absolutists and Democrats, by monarchs and mobs. When the Terrorists were daily sending to the guillotine hundreds of men and women, they ordered the lions, tigers, and hyenas of the great menagerie to be respected. They treated them as brethren. And when foreign troops occupied Paris in 1815, by special agreement, this wonderful place was protected from injury. I spent more time in these magnificent grounds and museums than at any other place in Paris.

I was greatly disappointed in Père la Chaise. It lies on a rising ground outside the wall of the city, and contains about 150 acres. It received its name from a Jesuit priest who once lived there, and was opened as a cemetery only in 1804. Its main approach is through an avenue lined on both sides with stone-cutters' shops, who have marble fashioned in all forms ready for lettering; and with retailers of wreaths, of all colors and sizes, for the decoration of the tombs of the departed. These retailers are very importunate in the sale of their chattels. You enter the grounds by a wide avenue, but are soon lost among the narrow paths that lead off in every direction. It is thick with stones and monuments, so as in many cases to render a passage between them impossible. The elegant tombs are but few, while the inelegant are in great numbers, and all of them holding up for perusal "boasting epitaphs," so as to impress you with the belief that none but the great, the virtuous, the heroic, and the pious found sepulture there. The tomb of Abelard and Heloise is a gem of its kind. There is a fine bust of Casimir Perier over his grave, which bears a striking likeness to that of our own lamented Webster. The grave of Marshal Ney, whose murder Wellington might have prevented, and whose not doing so is without excuse, is shown you, without a stone to tell the stranger whose ashes repose there. "Why," I asked the guide, "is there no monument to Ney?" "France is his monument," was the sentimental reply. We smile at the simplicity, not to say silliness, of the inscriptions which are often seen in our own rural grave-yards; but when you read upon the monuments in Père la Chaise such sentiments as these,

"*His widow continues his business, Rue Saint Denis*, 340."

"*Very high, very powerful princess, aged one day*"—one is ready to conclude that there are things to excite a smile out of America as well as in it.

The religion and frivolity of the French are both conspicuous in this far-famed cemetery. A Popish chapel is within the gate, where any body may have mass said "for a compensation." Crosses are upon the tombs of both saints and sinners. And frequently you are attracted by a small group looking through an iron grating into a tomb, where is an altar in the form of a lady's dressing table, with vases of flowers, sometimes natural, more frequently artificial, a gilt lamp, silver candlesticks, and all the usual et ceteras of a boudoir. This is French taste. And people crowd to see those things just as they crowd round the windows of taste and fashion in the Palais Royal. Save in the splendid views which you occasionally catch from its highest points, Père la Chaise is not to be compared in naturalness, taste, or beauty to Greenwood or Mount Auburn. It is in every respect inferior to the cemetery at Naples.

CHAPTER IX.

Nôtre Dame.—The Power of the Keys.—A Shaving Shop in a Cathedral.—Hôtel Dieu.—A Nun in a Circle.—Vincennes.—A Mistake.—Blame divided.—The Donjon.—Salle de la Question.—Justice will come.

I AM not yet out of Paris.

Nôtre Dame is the Cathedral of Paris—the historic church of France. It has its place in the bloody revolutions and persecutions of the country. It is on the "Isle de la Cité," and of course in the most ancient part of the city, and is conspicuous by its double Gothic towers. It was here that "Te Deums" were sung on the cruel murder of Protestants—that a courtesan was crowned as the Goddess of Reason during the frenzy of the Revolution—and that Napoleon placed the imperial crown on his own head, and that of Josephine, in 1804, in the presence of the Pope, and of an assemblage more brilliant than any Paris ever witnessed before or since. A star wrought in the marble marks the spot where he stood on that great occasion.

As you approach this pile of masonry you are struck with its dingy appearance—its antique bas-reliefs, and the magnificent circular window between the towers, said to be thirty feet in diameter. It is French in its appearance. Various hands and ages have had to do with it; and it is yet unfinished. We entered a side door into the tower, and soon the vast interior was before us. The floor is of marble. There are no seats.

Piles of split-bottom chairs with high backs are on either hand, which one can hire for a few sous at any time. On the sides are altars, and candles, and confession boxes; and we saw here and there an old woman or a young servant whispering confessions into the ear of a priest, whose face, whether from shame or wine, recalled the color of Burgundy. The grand altar is shut out from the body of the church by an iron railing, within which you can enter—"for a compensation." A silver or golden key has great efficacy within the dominions of Popery. It will open a church, or chapel, or relic box: it opens the gates of Paradise or Purgatory. Between the railing and the grand altar are some magnificent paintings. On either side of this altar, but shut out from it, are rooms which contain treasures and relics. In them we were shown the splendid robe in which Napoleon was crowned, priestly robes embroidered with gold, gifts of popes and kings made at different times to this old Cathedral, and, passing from the sublime to the ridiculous, the bullet which killed Affre, the archbishop of Paris, during the emeute of 1848!

As we passed round the building, we saw here and there poor, ragged devotees praying before pictures, counting their beads, and leaning over chairs. It appeared far more like a heathen than a Christian temple. As we were going out we passed a confessional where a female was confessing, and two others were waiting for their turn. "There is a shaving shop," said one of the company in broken English. Startled by the remark, and by hearing my own tongue, even in foreign accent, I joined conversation with the person. "Why call it a shaving shop?" said I. "They take money from the people for nothing, and seduce the women," was the reply. I found him to be a French merchant from New York, who had been brought up in the Papal Church, and who had seen enough of its priests to form a true estimate of them.

Nôtre Dame is inferior to St. Paul's or to Westminster Abbey. It is in an old and crowded part of the city, where nothing can be seen to advantage. Although the laying of its foundations dates back to the fabulous ages of remote antiquity, it is yet unfinished. It is in many respects a type of the Romish Church—it lifts itself high—it has much external pretension—it is dingy and faded—while internally it is empty, and cold, and damp. We were chilled there on a hot day; it was pleasant to get out into the air and sunshine.

Under the shadow of Nôtre Dame is the Hôtel Dieu, the most ancient hospital of Paris, whose foundations date back to the seventh century. It has been gradually enlarged by public and private benefactions, until it now contains upward of 800 beds. Here the sick and wounded are received, with the exception of children, incurable and insane persons, and those with cutaneous diseases. The yearly average of patients is 12,000, and the mortality one in eight. We were taken through it by an official wearing a chapeau militaire, and whose step indicated that he had often marched to the tap of the drum. There is one immense hall with three rows of beds, nearly all of which were filled with sick men. Every thing was perfectly neat—the rooms, beds, cooking, washing, waiting. Not an unpleasant odor was perceptible. Altars, candles, and crucifixes were offensively numerous. We saw here and there a lazy-looking priest confessing the sick ; the nuns were numerous. But the sight which most deeply impressed me was that of a circle of recovering invalids around a sister, who in a sweet and earnest manner was reading to them from a book. Our approach diverted the attention of some of them, but the nun read on. I did not approach near enough to see the book, or to hear any of its contents. But it did not look like a Bible—probably not a copy of it is to be found in the building—and I suppose she was reading to them from the Lives of the Saints, that miserable fabrication of lying legends and old wives' fables, by which the priests would every where supplant the Word of God. These poor nuns are every where the dupes of the priests, when they are nothing worse. The Hôtel Dieu bore to us a much greater resemblance to the house of God than does the Nôtre Dame under whose shadow it reclines.

We made quite an unexpected visit one morning to Vincennes, outside the wall of the city, and famous in history as a royal residence, and for its being a prison of state, and now one of the strongest fortifications in the kingdom or *empire*. We started for Versailles, and were put down at Vincennes. So much for our bad French and the roguery of the coacher. He insisted that we said Vincennes instead of Versailles, and we thought he lied about it to get our money. But we also thought, as the fare was paid, the best plan was to divide the blame—to charge half the mistake to our French, and the other half to his falsehood, and to act like heroes. Yet there before us was the Donjon where the gallant Henry V. of England reigned and died—

which was converted into a prison by Louis VI.—where the Duke d'Enghien was murdered in 1804—where Polignac, minister of Charles X., was imprisoned in 1830—and where yet is to be seen the "*Salle de la Question,*" with its fearful bed, upon which men were tortured during the application of the "Question." Heaven only knows the cruelties committed within that Donjon, through those long years when French kings perpetrated crimes by "*lettres de cachet,*" which are a disgrace to humanity. We almost forgive the roguery of the driver, who, to get a shilling out of strangers, took us to Vincennes, as we had thus an opportunity of gazing upon a place so famous in history, and upon that Donjon that has had such a baptism of blood. It would seem as if the spirits of the multitudes there murdered were hovering around its turrets, waiting the arrival of that retributive justice which, though slowly, will surely come.

CHAPTER X.

Versailles. — The Palace. — Picture Gallery. — Chapel. — Theatre. — Banqueting Room. — Room of Louis XIV. — Room of Death. — Room where was signed the Revocation of the Edict of Nantz. — The Balcony. — The Gardens. — Whence the Revenues. — Causes of the Revolution. — Bourbon Dynasty. — Moral Lessons of Versailles.

I AM yet in Paris, and am telling what I saw.

We started again for Versailles, determined this time to reach it. We walked to the "Chemin de fer," and after whirling us around the city, we were dropped in the heart of the town in half an hour. We met in the cars a British officer, retired on half-pay, who had been often there, who spoke the French as a native, and who kindly offered to take us around the place. So intelligent was he, and so thoroughly conversant with the town and the palace, that we saw all that was to be seen in the day, under the very best circumstances. The town itself is old and decaying, having once had a population of 100,000, and now reduced to less than 30,000. But of the palace, what can I say?

It is a monument to the taste, the extravagance, to the pride and folly of the voluptuous Louis XIV. Some idea may be formed of its surpassing splendor, of its buildings, gardens, fountains, waterfalls, statuary, and paintings, when it is known that it cost about forty millions sterling, and that 30,000 soldiers, when they could be spared from the battle-field, were simultaneously employed on the works! The palace is approached by a very wide avenue, amid statuary, fountains, and soldiers. At eleven o'clock you gain admittance, and may wander amid its numberless apartments as you please. There are the great picture galleries, the finest in the world, where, in historical paintings, the great battles of kings, emperors, and republicans are placed before you. You wander over acres of canvas, glowing with the finest creations of the great masters, until oppressed by the feelings of pleasure and wonder. There is the magnificent *Chapel*, with its gilded furniture, where royal sinners went to mass; and where royal courtesans went to confession, and where each could secure from a pliant and profligate priesthood pardon for the past and indulgence for the future. And there, before that altar, stood the beautiful Maria Antoinette, when she was wedded to Louis XVI., in 1769. And there is the *Salle de l' Opéra*, where the Bourbon court, sparkling in jewels and diamonds, and amid the blaze of ten thousand wax candles, crowded to attend theatrical exhibitions. The stage was now vacant, and I sat down in the very seat where the beautiful queen of the Sixteenth Louis, whose tragic end made the world weep, often reclined, attracting all eyes and hearts to herself. And this is the very place whither the court fled for counsel on that fearful hour, when that furious mob reached the gates, which marched out from Paris to wreak their vengeance upon their royal oppressors. And there is the grand Banqueting Room, less than three hundred feet long, the finest in the world, where Louis displayed all the grandeur of royalty, and all the luxury of his times, and where were given the most splendid fêtes of Europe. But profound quiet had now succeeded to royal revelry.

Every room in this magnificent royal abode has its history. There is the very chair and table of Louis XIV., and in the room where he planned most of his great wars and battles—where Louis XV. signed the decree expelling the Jesuits—where his bold and impudent mistress, Du Barri, who died by the guillotine, in the presence of his ministers snatched from his hands a package of letters and threw them into the fire; and where Louis XVI. received the reply sent by Mirabeau, that the Assembly would not adjourn save at the point of his bayonets!

And here is the room where Louis the Great died, bewailing his sins, and terrified, as well he might be, in view of the judgment; and where Louis XV. died of small-pox, hated of all men, and with one watcher, an old woman, who announced his death by the putting out a candle in the window of his room! What a just termination of a cruel and profligate life!

And here is the room where the infamous Jesuits, La Chaise and La Tellier, secured the revocation of the Edict of Nantz. Bloody men of a hated order! God save us from their wiles!

And there is the balcony, on which I gazed with emotions of horror, where Maria Antoinette appeared at the call of the mob which filled the court below, yelling for vengeance. When she was married, a fearful thunder storm threw Versailles and the surrounding country into terror—it was regarded as an omen of her fearful end! And there is the room into which the mob had broken but a few moments after her escape, and into whose bed they plunged a hundred daggers. Her murder is the bloodiest chapter in the bloody history of the bloody revolution. As I gazed upon that balcony, I thought I could see her in loveliness, with her children on either side of her, facing the fury of the mob, which recoiled for a moment, with a murmur of admiration, at her presence; and on my return to Paris, I imagined I could see her spirit hovering over that city, and crying, in view of the delay of justice, "How long! O Lord, how long!"

On leaving the palace for the gardens and parks which lie in the rear, you enter a scene of fairy enchantment which can not be described. Groves, lawns, serpentine walks, lanes, waterfalls, parterres of flowers, fountains, and statuary, bewilder you with their number, opulence, beauty, and magnificence. I doubt whether of its kind there is a sight in the world to be compared to the view from the wall which surmounts the orangery in the garden of Versailles.

But whence the immense revenues required to produce, amid the wild forest, magnificence like this? The very stables are palaces, and the horses of the Bourbons were better cared for than the princes of other lands! And whence the revenues that created and sustained such splendid and profuse royalty? They were wrung from the peasantry and citizens, who were regarded by that bad race of kings as does a farmer his cattle, who are reared to yield their milk and beef for his profit! The French people saw and felt how they were ground to sustain royal profligates and prostitutes, and they waited their time of vengeance! The Revolution was onlv the effect of the outpouring of the wrath of the nation, which had been accumulating for ages under the pressure of the iron heel of despotism. And when men and women seemed equally savage, it is to be remembered they were equally oppressed. Some of the causes which led to the bloodiest revolution in the annals of time, you see in the fading magnificence of Versailles.

And, were I a Frenchman, there is nothing which gave a hope of preventing it which I would not do, to prevent the return of the Bourbon dynasty. Taken as a whole, it was a cruel one; with scarcely an exception, its kings were vain, oppressive, tyrannical, superstitious, lascivious, and cruel. Louis XIV. was the most regal of them all—the flower of the race. And yet no right mind can form an acquaintance with his interior history without holding him in royal contempt. To see him scorning his wife—caressing his mistresses—sending his favorite of to-day into exile to-morrow—living daily in open debauchery—going to bed at night with a scapular and crucifix to keep off the devil—rising and dressing amid a silly formalism, the very recital of which fills you with disgust—sipping his coffee and wine—then going to prayers amid his attendants—then going to mass amid bishops and cardinals who were ever singing hosannas to the royal saint—shedding the blood of his people like water, and then dying amid the horrors which the recollection of his sins and profligacy could not fail to excite—O, if this was the flower of the Bourbon race, may France be ever free from their rule, and the world from their example!

The moral lesson and instructions to be learned at Versailles are very many and very important. The race of monarchs that expended millions in its erection are now banished and detested. The halls, once crowded with the great and the noble of Europe, and resounding with their revelry, are now silent. And those oaken floors, waxed and polished so brightly as almost to reflect your image, and upon which none but royal or noble feet were permitted to tread, are now daily trod by peasants and by strangers from other lands, who resort there to gaze upon the beauties of art, and the effects of the creative skill of man. Versailles is now only a national gallery! "Sic transit gloria mundi."

CHAPTER XI.

Bastile.—Lettres de Cachet.—Man of Iron Mask.—Column of July.—Emeute of 1848.—Place de la Concord.—Obelisk of Luxor.—Guillotine.—January 21st and October 16th, 1793.—National Assembly Hall.—Confusion.—Republicanism dishonored.

Yet in Paris.

The Place de la Bastile is one of great historic interest. It is an open space whence many streets radiate, and in the centre of which rises the famous *Column of July*. Here once stood the Bastile, formerly a famous castle, in which state prisoners, arrested by *lettres de cachet*, were confined. By these "lettres" a man was taken from his family for any or no reason, and was carried none knew whither. They were usually plunged into the cells of this building. If a man knew any thing whose revelation might be injurious to king, or minister, or mistress, here was his home! What days of tyranny have passed over our world! Here was confined "the man with iron mask," about whom so much has been written, and as to whom curiosity is yet on tip-toe. He was treated with the highest distinction—was fed by the hand of the chief keeper—was denied nothing he desired—but ever wore an iron mask, behind which no eye was permitted to look. He made, it is said, two efforts to reveal his confinement to the world. Once he threw a shirt out of the window on which he had written something. It was picked up by a priest, who took it to the keeper without reading what was written. The priest, *lest he should have read it*, was put to death. Once he threw a silver plate out of the window upon which he had scratched something. It was found by a peasant and given back to the keeper. "Have you read what is here written?" said the keeper. "I can not read," was the reply. Having satisfied himself that the man could not read, the keeper dismissed him, saying, "You are very fortunate in not knowing how to read." Among many conjectures in reference to him, some intimate that he was a twin brother of Louis XIV., and that he was thus disposed of to prevent civil wars, as the twins might put in equal claims for the throne. If the true history of the Bastile could be written, tyranny, treachery, blood, and murder would mark its every page.

It was captured by the people in July, 1789. In the following year it was demolished by order of the Assembly, and where it stood now stands the Column of July, 150 feet high, inscribed all over with the names of the martyrs of liberty, surmounted by a ball, on which stands a colossal gilt figure of the Genius of Liberty, standing on one foot, holding a torch in one hand and a broken chain in the other, with wings expanded ready to fly away. If it remains there yet, since the tricks of Louis Napoleon, it must be made of bronze or of brass.

Here were the strongest barricades of the insurgents of June, 1848. It was here that the most fearful contest of that emeute took place. The marks of it are visible on nearly all the surrounding houses. And it was here that Affre, archbishop of Paris, was killed, attempting to persuade the insurgents to desist. It was on the pavement that surrounds the Monument that the throne of the Bourbons was consumed.

Between the garden of the Tuileries and the Champs Elysées, and between the Madeleine and the Chamber of Deputies, lies the "Place de la Concorde." It is beautiful for situation. This was formerly the "Place de la Révolution." Here stands the magnificent monument of ancient Egypt, the Obelisk of Luxor, which stood before the temple of Thebes fifteen centuries before the birth of Christ, and which was raised to its present position in 1836, in the presence of Louis Philippe and his court, and such a crowd as Paris can give for such an occasion. And here are fountains, and statuary, and magnificence on every hand, to attract your gaze and call forth your admiration. But, as I walked over these enchanting grounds, recollections of other days came over me. Here was erected the revolutionary guillotine, a machine invented in Italy, and imported into France by a humane physician, Guillotin, whence its name, for the purpose of superseding the inhuman and atrocious methods of taking life. On the 21st of January, 1793, the Bridge de la Concorde, the terraces of the Tuileries, the parapets on the border of the river, the tops of all the surrounding houses, the leafless trees in the Champs Elysées, and all these open grounds, were densely crowded with an excited people. A carriage drove up to the guillotine. A man of noble mien was led out of it. His hands were bound, and he was laid on the plank—the blade fell, and the head of Louis XVI. rolled in the dust! An executioner took it by the hair, and held it up to the view of the bloodthirsty crowd. Cruel Frenchmen jumped on the scaffold, and, dipping the points of their swords in the royal blood flowing around them, and waving them toward heaven, cried out, "Vive la République!" O France, France!

A few months have passed away, and on the 16th of October of the same year, another and similar crowd is collected in the same place. An open cart, used to carry the lowest criminals to death, slowly makes its way amid hissing crowds of men and women —the women the most coarse in their abuse—and stops before the guillotine. A female, with a white gown soiled and crumpled, with her ringlets fallen over her face and neck, descends from it. Her mouth sorrowfully preserved the folds of royal pride, which no suffering could tame, and which nothing could hide. She was bound to the plank, and the blade fell—and the head of Maria Antoinette, the Queen of France, the daughter of the Emperor Francis I. and of Maria Theresa, rolled away from its body! The executioner took it by the hair, and went the round of the scaffold with it, raising it up in his hand, showing it to the people, who raised a long, loud cry of "Vive la République!" And the most furious in Paris for the life of this queen, and those who showed the most frantic joy on her execution, were women. O France, France!

And here I was treading the very ground on which the guillotine stood, where rivers of blood were shed, and where those scenes, which to this hour shock and sadden the civilized world, were enacted! And now it is called *Place de la Concorde*, and is a place of enchanting beauty! And yet it is steeped in blood!

From this bloody and beautiful spot, you cross the

Seine by a magnificent bridge, built in part by stone from the demolished Bastile, and fronting you on the opposite bank stands the Hall of the National Assembly, with its Grecian portico and twelve Corinthian columns. With an embassador's ticket I entered it from the rear, and was shown by officials to the gallery to which such tickets give admission. The Assembly was in full blast. Dupin sat as president, a large, full man, with semi-bald head, full face, and more English than French in appearance. Behind him sat two men, for what purpose I did not learn. They helped him to keep order! A little stand, the tribune, like to a chorister's desk in a Scotch church, was before him. And on the seats, rising from the centre on all sides, amphitheatre like, sat the members. They were numerous, and gentlemanly in appearance. Every speaker went to the tribune. A deputy ascended, buttoned to his chin, gloved, and brushed in true French style. He spoke calmly, and showed his gloves to perfection. The point in debate was about some duty on sugar. He uttered a sentence with force, and a cry was heard from a deputy, and another, and another; and soon the house was in a perfect uproar. The orator folded his gloved hands on his bosom, and stood calm, as if made of marble, until the tumult subsided. He went on again, and soon the storm returned with fourfold violence. Members shouted, jumped to their feet, and brandished their arms in the air. I supposed there was to be a fight at once. Again the speaker stood quiet, and again the storm subsided. He resumed again, and the storm howled with still greater fury. Dupin hammered the desk, the men above him ringing a bell; and such a Babel, for fifteen or twenty minutes, I never saw before or since. The man descended from the tribune, and the vote was taken; and as they passed to and fro, voting, talking, and scolding, they seemed to me the most excitable set of human beings that ever was created. To this excitement there were some exceptions. The ministers of Louis Napoleon, who sat near the centre of the room, and on the lowest seats, moved not. Nor did Cavaignac, a man of middle stature, serious aspect, simple dress, who sat thoughtful among his brethren.

If this was their usual way of legislating, I did not wonder when Louis Napoleon sent them home. One master is better than a million such, even when that master is "the nephew of his uncle." Many heads sometimes make a hydra—of which there is some proof in American as well as French history. The French Assembly disgraced Republicanism in Europe. France has no religion and no fixed principles, and as long as the alternative is between socialism and despotism, no man who has *any thing* at stake will long hesitate as to his choice. My sense of shame, because of the scenes which occasionally disgrace our legislative chambers at Washington, was somewhat relieved by my visit to the National Assembly. If the American people only knew the use which is made abroad of the vulgar and shameful conduct of some of our senators and representatives in our halls of legislation, to prop up despotic institutions, and to bring republicanism into contempt, they would prevent our brawlers from disgracing our country by voting them the privilege of staying at home.

CHAPTER XII.

Sabbath in Paris.—Madeleine.—Toupet.—The Interior.—Le Suisse. —Appearance and Duties.—A Funeral.—A young Couple at Mass. —Sights Seen.—High Mass.—Bad Influence of Popery on Paris.

A Sabbath day spent in Paris, where there is no Sabbath set apart to the service of God by the people, is not easily forgotten by a Protestant! And it is impossible so to describe it as to make a person who never witnessed it fully to comprehend it. Popery in Papal countries knows no Sabbath; in Paris it has converted it into the harvest day of play-actors, shop-keepers, restaurants, buffoons, and mountebanks.

The Madeleine is an exquisite building, Grecian in its form and proportions. It was designed by Bonaparte as a Temple of Glory to the French arms, but is now a Papal Church. It is surrounded on all sides by fifty-two Corinthian columns, and is lighted entirely from above. It is both externally and internally gorgeously decorated by sculpture and paintings, and has cost nearly three millions of dollars. It is the most gorgeous and fashionable place of Papal worship in the city. From its southern portico a view of great beauty lies before you, as your eyes wander with delight over the Place de la Concorde, the bridges over the Seine, and the hall of the National Assembly.

Desirous to see the practical workings of Popery, I visited this building many times. On entering it from the southern porch, you are soon arrested by a railing with a gate in the centre of it. At this gate stood the most dry, wrinkled, and insignificant looking person I ever saw in the form of a man, holding at the end of a short handle a brush wet with holy water. He was very old, very ugly, with a nose twice as long as necessary, very small, very stupid-looking, and with a cap on his head rising like a sugar-loaf. He is called, I believe, the "Toupet," from his holding out the brush. The faithful, as they enter, most daintily touch the brush with their gloved fingers, and cross themselves. This, of course, I declined; and the little fellow's eyes seemed for a moment to assume an expression of fear that I might be an unbeliever in the sanctifying efficacy of touching his brush. If I were called upon to draw the picture of an incarnate male witch, I would select for my model the Toupet of the Madeleine.

After passing the door guarded by the above relic of antiquity, you are surrounded by splendid paintings and statuary. The high altar is before you; confession boxes and altars are on either hand; there are no pews or seats; and if you wish to sit or pray, you can have a split-bottom chair for a few sous, which are piled up on all sides. Your attention is soon arrested by the stately movements of another official, called "Le Suisse." He was in every respect a fine contrast to the Toupet. He was at least six feet two, with broad shoulders, and dressed as a field-marshal. He wore a chapeau militaire, side-arms, white tights, gloves, and carried an immense halbert in one hand, and an immense cane in the other. He seemed the most self-satisfied being I ever saw. He goes all over the house at pleasure, and stands by the altar, even when the priest is making God out of a wafer, without any apparent reverence. When all others are uncovered and on their knees, this official walks about as stately as ever, without even a nod of respect to host or priest. This fine-looking fellow, that I first supposed to be some famed general or commodore come hither to make a votive offering to Mary or Mars, is a mere servant, who leads the priests to the altars and leads them away; who makes way for the monks or priests through the crowd when taking up collections; who stands godfather for all children baptized who have no fathers; and who says "Amen" at funerals when there are none else to respond. I never before saw so big a man engaged in such small business. And yet he threw all the priests in the shade, attracting to himself the attention of all strangers. If I had the ear of the priests, I would advise them to dismiss that stately "Suisse" if they wish strangers to notice themselves or their pantomime. I would know him if I met him in the moon, while the priests, like sheep or geese, seemed all alike.

I went to the Madeleine several times during the week. I witnessed a marriage at one of its altars, and a funeral at another. I was there when the poor and when the fashionable go to mass. And the more frequently I went, the more I was impressed with the utter heartlessness of Popery. A coffin made of very disjointed boards, kept together by ropes, was brought in and laid before an altar. After some time the Suisse came clattering along with the priest behind him. A ceremony was mumbled hurriedly over, of which I could not hear a word but the response of the knight of the halbert, and then the poor people took away their dead!

A spruce young couple came to mass, smelling strongly of musk, as I can testify. The young lady knelt on the bottom of a chair, hid her face for a few moments, and then, yet kneeling, commenced a talk with her friend, who stood, hat and cane in hand, by the chair. And thus they spent some twenty minutes—she alternately praying, talking, and laughing, and the man, when she was praying, looking with an opera-glass upon the persons and things around him. And this is the manner of the fashionable Parisians at mass. It is a frivolous alternation of giggle and praying, of praying and giggle, which proves beyond all question the utter absence of the mind and heart from the service.

On Sabbath morning the sun rose warm, and without a cloud, over the city of Paris. I felt I was from home, and in a Papal country. After breakfast, and worship with a few friends in an upper room, we went to the Madeleine to witness high mass. As we went along the Rue Rivoli, masons were at work on the streets and public buildings, supervised by an officer in livery; shops were every where open, and more attractively decorated than usual; soldiers were marching and counter-marching along the streets, and across the Place de la Concorde, and in nothing did the town differ from the other days in the week, save in the gayer dress of the people, the greater appearance of finery in the shops, the greater number of purchasers, the increased number of soldiers, and the more densely crowded state of all the fashionable promenades. We made our way to the church.

As we approached its splendid southern portico, people were coming out in considerable numbers, while others were entering. We entered, passed the Toupet, whose skin looked as if it was borrowed from a mummy, and hired chairs. Mass soon opened, and the drama was acted very well. The bishop and priests were in full attire; twice, followed by priests shaking their boxes, did the stately Suisse parade the entire church, asking alms from the people. And amid the noise of his cane, halbert, and heels upon a marble floor; of the changing of money to pay for the chairs occupied by the people; of the jingling of their boxes by the priests, to give notice of their approach; of the ringing of bells from the altar; of the deep tones of the noble organ, which swelled one after another through the ample building; of the talking of the young, and of the whispering of strangers, of whom there seemed to be many, the reader may judge of the wership we were enabled to render to Him who requires his creatures to worship Him in spirit and in truth. Candles, statuary, painting, priests dressed in the most gorgeous style of man-millinery, were there in profusion; but there were no religious emotions, no worship of God, no religious instruction. And we retired from the gorgeous scene, feeling that, if that were the worship which the High and Lofty One required from intelligent creatures, God and religion were both a farce. No wonder that a religion, of which this is the highest style, does so little to instruct the people, or to render Paris a moral city. The judgment day will reveal how much of the blood that has so often deluged this city—how much of its crimes and dissoluteness—how much of the influence for evil which it exerts on Europe and on the world, will be found on the skirts, and required at the hands of Popery and its priests.

CHAPTER XIII.

A pleasant Meeting in the Madeleine.—Wesleyan Chapel.—The Service.—"Clothes."—Minister for Paris.—Prayer-meeting.—Sabbath Evening Walk.—Sights seen.—Reasons for French Character.—The Riddle solved.—A Look at St. Germain.—A Prayer.

I AM yet describing a Sabbath in Paris.

When the mummery of high mass in the Madeleine was drawing to a close—when the Suisse, with military tread and martial air, commenced, for the second time, making a pathway for the priests who followed, rattling their boxes, and asking for money, we rose to depart. We gave once, and did not care to pay again, even for such magnificent nonsense. On turning round we were most happy to meet an honorable judge and honored Christian from Pennsylvania, with his reverend son—a clergyman from Boston, and a gentleman from Providence. Although comparatively strangers, we soon felt that we were friends. Were it not for this casual meeting, I might not have seen Rome. How sweet to meet Christian friends and fellow-citizens in a foreign land!

At twelve, we went together to the Wesleyan Chapel in the Rue Madeleine, and almost under the shadow of the splendid church which we had just left. We entered by a narrow alley. The room is small, but it was well filled, and mostly with men. Soon a man of good appearance, of comparative youth, and of serious aspect, entered the pulpit, and without robes. His accent was strongly English. The Episcopal service was read by him from the beginning to the end, just as I had heard it in St. James's, Westminster, with the prayers "for our beloved Queen Victoria, her royal consort Prince Albert," the royal children and all. The whole thing struck me strangely. Why these prayers in France for England's royal family? Why this slavish use of the prayer-book by a Methodist clergyman in Paris? And never did I see so much the need of robes on the minister, and responses from the people, to make the formulary of the prayer-book tolerable. When well read, and with hearty responses, I have been edified by it; but on this occasion it was oppressive. The constant repetition of the same forms, as Carlyle would say, "needs clothes" to render them tolerable. Without gowns, responses, and frequent down-sittings and up-risings, the prayer-book would be soon laid aside. So I judged from the effect of its naked and unvaried perusal upon myself on this occasion. But "clothes" are essential to the continuance of many other things as well as the Prayer-book.

The minister preached from the thirtieth chapter of Isaiah, and the thirty-third verse, a sermon on the doctrine of future punishment. It struck me as a most inappropriate and feeble effort. The room was filled with strangers from Britain and America, and who went there from the husks of Popery to be fed with the Gospel. Many, I know, were disappointed. And yet, inappropriate and feeble as was the effort, and destitute as was the preacher of emotion, the service was incomparably better than the hocus pocus, in all its gorgeous drapery, which we had just witnessed in the Madeleine.

The importance of a first-rate American preacher of the Gospel in Paris can not be too highly estimated. Such is now the facility of transatlantic travel, that the number of those must be constantly on the increase who will seek their summer recreations in Europe. And a noble preacher, of fervent heart and piety, meeting such in Paris, would be to them as a stream in the desert, as the shadow of a great rock in a weary land. Why is not such a minister of God there?

Before we left the Wesleyan Chapel, we projected a service of our own; and at four o'clock we met in the Hotel Windsor, in a private room, for reading the Scriptures and for prayer. The number which met in the Madeleine was increased by the addition of the Rev. Dr. C. and his three fine boys. A more pleasant meeting I never attended. There we were in a foreign land, surrounded by people of a strange tongue, some of us away from our people, and all of us from our families and homes, and in the midst of a people proverbially estranged from God. And the word of the Lord was sweet to our taste; and we prayed, weeping, for our people, our families, our home. That meeting for prayer in Paris on the Sabbath afternoon will not be soon forgotten by any that were there!

As the light of the Sabbath's sun commenced waning in the sky, and when the mild, balmy air of evening had succeeded to the rather oppressive heat of the day, we went forth to see for ourselves the way in which the Sabbath evening is kept in Paris. We went from the palace of the Tuileries, through its garden, and the Place de la Concorde, and the Champs Elysées. Thence we turned into the Boulevards, and through the Rue

Richelieu home. And such sights I never beheld! It would seem as if all Paris had turned into the streets. Here were soldiers marching in platoons; there was ballad-singing under a canopy, surrounded by people sitting on benches and sipping wines and ices. Here were elegantly dressed girls dancing; and there was a crowd collected around gamboling monkeys. Here was a man selling trinkets at auction, and there were gambling tables. Here were a few women going to church, and there were crowds of men and women rushing to the theatre and opera. The Boulevards were densely crowded; the shops were all open—their windows surrounded by admiring spectators; and at short intervals the sidewalks were covered with tables, around which men and women sat, in the open air, regaling themselves with wines and confectionery. Occasionally you would come to a stand in the Champs Elysées where men were playing all kinds of mountebank tricks, surrounded by hundreds of admiring spectators. The restaurants seemed crowded by men, women, and children. Not a vestige of evidence to remind you of the Sabbath was any place apparent. The whole route taken through the city wore the appearance of a Fourth of July in New York, when booths were allowed around the Park. The proof was positive that Paris at least has no religion. And it is very remarkable to what an extent the manner in which the Sabbath is kept is a type of the moral character of a people, and of a man. A Parisian Sabbath is as certain an index to the character of the French, as is a Sabbath in Edinburgh to the character of the Scotch.

After visiting its churches during the day, and taking the walk above described on Sabbath evening, you no longer wonder at the character which Paris has in all the earth. The wealth of the Church is spent in fostering the arts; the labors of the clergy are expended in vain ceremonies; there is no instruction from the pulpit; and all the efforts of the priests are directed, not to enlighten the people in the knowledge of God, not to purify the heart, but to gratify the senses. A church is more or less attractive according to its wealth, its pictures, its statuary, or its relics in the way of old bones from the catacombs of Rome or Naples. And people resort to them, not to worship God, but in accordance to custom, or as they would resort to an opera or to an exhibition of the arts. The frivolous character of the religion of France is obvious even amid their most solemn ceremonials; for I have seen the women on their knees during the elevation of the host, praying, laughing, talking; now turning their eyes on the ground; now raising them most piously on a picture; and now turning them laughingly on their lovers or friends, without ever changing their kneeling position!

French character is a riddle. You meet the French in the garden of the Tuileries, gay, joyous, with hearts light as down, and in the Champs Elysées, as full of fun, frolic, and dance as you can conceive. So polite are they, that in cases where an Englishman would pass on without uttering a word, they will turn upon you with hat off, bowing most reverently, and asking a thousand pardons. You would not, you could not, impute to them any thing but a joyous, polite, and refined character; and yet to-morrow those very persons, men and women, may be furies, covered with scars, ragged, half naked, caring neither for God or man, carrying a rapier in one hand and a tri-colored flag in the other, and wading ankle deep in blood, to gratify their thirst for more. They will raise barricades—scale walls—face cannon—demolish prisons—burn thrones, churches, or palaces—guillotine kings and queens, and shed their own blood like water, to indulge the excitement of the hour. And why thus? Why so refined, polite, sympathizing one day, and so demoniacal the next? The French are morally uneducated. Sentiment, passion, the outward, are every thing with them. They are versatile, inflammable, and atheistic in the undertone of their opinions. Popery is an overcoat to put off or on as suits the hour. And when their passions are up, there is no great principle to guide them; there is nothing in time or eternity to fear; and they rush on like a raging tornado, blind as the winds. With the religious training and principles of Scotland, the French would be the noblest people on the globe. The grand want of France is religion, and this is a want which Popery can never supply.

On my Sabbath evening stroll through Paris, I stood for a few minutes before the church St. Germain l'Auxerrois. As I gazed upon its belfry, my thoughts recurred to that dreadful period, the 23d of August, 1572, when its bell gave the signal for the awful massacre of St. Bartholomew, and tolled the death-knell of the Protestants of France through the whole night, while the hired assassins of court, bishops, and priests were butchering Coligny and his fellow-Protestants!

With a shudder of horror, I turned away from the sight and went home. O Popery, the blood of the millions thou hast slain is pleading against thee before the throne of eternal justice! False in principle, fanatical in spirit, and ferocious in heart, may the Lord soon destroy thee with the brightness of his rising!

CHAPTER XIV.

Exit from Paris.—A Diligence.—Beaune.—Chalons.—Abelard and Heloise.—Face of the Country.—French Villages.—The Peasantry.—The Saone.—Ladies' Dress.—Old Habits retained.—American Peculiarity.—A Digression.

Having spent what time we had to spare in Paris, we started for Italy by the way of Lyons and Marseilles. We were packed into a diligence at the Messageries Générales, Rue St. Honoré. This is a traveling concern which can scarcely be described to a person that has not seen it. It contains four kinds of places—the coupé in front, the best and dearest; the intérieur, or middle apartment; the rotonde, or hinder; and the banquette, on the top of the vehicle. The seats are all numbered, and your receipt informs the conducteur where to place you. Thus all scrambling for seats is prevented. It will hold fifteen or twenty persons. There is any amount of baggage on the top. It is a far more comfortable conveyance than any would take it to be at first sight. In one of these coaches we were driven out of the city to the railway depôt, when it was swung bodily from the wheels by a crane, and placed on the railway car, all retaining their seats. We were yoked to the iron steam-horse, and away we went through a level country, the beautiful woods and village of Fontainebleau, to Tonnerre, then the terminus of the "chemin de fer." There we were again swung on to the wheels of a coach, and yoked to two tier of horses, three abreast; we trundled along at the rate of six or seven miles an hour, day and night, to Beaune. We were dropped a little after daylight at, I presume, the best hotel in the town; but every thing looked so uncared-for that I called for eggs. If fresh, I knew they would be clean. After as much of breakfast as surrounding circumstances would permit us to take, we spent a few hours in viewing the old town. Here is the noble hospital of Nicholas Rollin, once chancellor to the Duke of Burgundy; here, also, is a college, which seemed neglected; here are strong ramparts, planted with trees, which form a magnificent promenade; but the chief celebrity of the town is owing to its being the centre of trade in the wine to which it gives its name, which is a species of the Burgundy. Julien says that the wines of Beaune have the justly acquired reputation of being "le plus francs de goût de toute la Bourgogne."

By railway we proceeded from Beaune to Chalons, on the Saone, which we reached in a short time. This was for many years the capital of the ancient kingdom of Burgundy, and is yet a place of considerable business. The streets seemed dirty, and the place looked as if it might be unhealthy. It is low, marshy, and the country very level. It was here the famous Abelard died in 1142, whose varied and romantic history is yet a subject of interest to the world. His intrigues with Heloise show to what an extent passion and religion, faith and falsehood, love and monkery, were mixed and mingled in the lives of the ecclesiastics of the Middle Ages. Heloise begged his body after his death, and had it buried in her own monastery, with the view of reposing in death by his side. In 1800 the ashes of both of them were removed to the Museum of French monuments at Paris, and the exquisite monument in Père la Chaise is erected to both of them, as the martyrs of love! At Chalons we took a steamer down the Saone to Lyons.

In this ride from north to south we had a fine opportunity of seeing the country portions of France. In the main, the face of the country is very level, and is well cultivated. The people live in villages, and neither horses nor cattle are seen dispersed over the country, as in Britain or with us. If now and then you see a cow feeding by the wayside, it has always an attendant to keep it within bounds. There are no fences to be seen any where; and lines of trees, running for miles without deviating from a straight line, constantly present themselves, until the eye is weary of seeing them. Where nothing richer can grow, the vine is sure to be planted. The hills are all vine-clad, and are often prettily terraced for its cultivation. The vines are planted about as far apart as are our hills of corn: the old stump seemed only a foot or two high, and the branches from the stump are only permitted to grow four or five feet long. Thus the strength of the tree is thrown into the fruit, instead of being permitted to expend itself in the production of long branches and many leaves. Vineyards thus cultivated were every where to be seen. They ran up the sides of the most steep acclivities, and capped the summit of the highest hills. Because they can stick a vine any where, the entire surface of the country is producing something.

The villages through which we passed present a very

strong contrast to our American villages. The streets are so narrow as often to make it impossible for two carriages to pass one another. The houses are built directly on the street, without door-yard or pavement in front. Sometimes the horses are eating on the first floor, while you are dining or supping on the second. And the air of neatness, cleanliness, comfort, which is worn by our best American villages, is generally absent from those of France.

The peasantry also seemed uncultivated, and in a low state of civilization. Women were every where working in the fields, and were doing all kinds of manual labor. And all along a canal, on the borders of which we traveled many miles, men were drawing the boats. The women seemed to be doing the work of men, and men the work of horses. In countries which support large standing armies, the men are needed for arms, for the deadly breach, as food for the cannon; hence the cultivation of the country must, of necessity, devolve upon women, if it is done at all. And, as we shall narrate by-and-by, we have seen men directing gangs of women in the field, as it is said drivers superintend gangs of negroes in some of our Southern plantations. When there, France was a republic, and yet soldiers were met every where. The people willed a republic, and legions of armed men were needed to induce the people to respect it! What a riddle are the French people!

The sail down the Saone to Lyons was very fine. The steamers on these rivers are very narrow and very long, and with very little to interrupt a promenade from stem to stern. We stopped at many places to give out and take in passengers, which was done adroitly and rapidly. At one place we took on board several females with head-dresses which excited the wonder of those of us who were travelers and strangers. Their bonnets I then likened to a large circular mat with a thimble placed on the centre of it. The thimble was placed over the head, and the leaf was tied on by very wide and gorgeous ribbons. Their nether garments were very short, and their shoes quite in the masculine order. I asked the captain who these strange-looking persons were, who told me that they were very respectable ladies of the place, wearing the dress peculiar to that locality.

There is nothing which strikes an American traveler in Europe more strongly than the attachment to old habits, fashions, and forms every where visible. The guides through the Tower of London are dressed as harlequins. The Lord Chancellor of England is buried in an enormous wig, with sleeves. The advocates pleading in court must wear their gown and wig. Welch-women wear hats like men. The people in many of the departments of France are distinguished by their dresses. They will tell you in Rome to what village the people from the country belong by the fashion of their garments. Mountains, and rivers, and often imaginary lines divide kingdoms, nations, and tongues. On one side of a river you find one set of customs; on the other, a very different set. On one side of a mountain you hear the Italian; on the other, the German, or the French, or a patois peculiar to the people. The British Channel is some twenty miles wide, and how different the people, the language, the religion on either side of it. In a few hours you may fly from Liverpool to Wales and to the Isle of Man, and these hours bring you among a people who speak the English, the Welsh, the Manx languages. This all seems singular to us, who can travel from east to west, and from north to south, over a country thousands of miles in extent, and find among all our people the same language, customs, and habits. These distinctions tend to keep up old jealousies, to foster prejudices, to retain the dividing lines of races and religions, and thus to obstruct the march of civilization and Christianity. They form strings upon which kings, princes, and priests can play so as to suit their own purposes. The people of Europe need to be shaken together, and to be kept together long enough, as it were in some chemical retort, in which they would lose their peculiarities, and from which they would come forth one people. The great peculiarity of our country is that we take all the varying people from all the varying nations of Europe, and cast them into our mill, and they come out in the grist, speaking our language, Americans and Protestants.

What a digression, caused by those curiously dressed women seen on our way from Chalons to Lyons!

CHAPTER XV.

The Saone.—Lyons: its Appearance—its History.—Peter de Vaud. —Revolutionary Scenes.—Precy.—Couthon.—Collot d'Herbois.— Horrid Murders by Jacobins.—Festoons of Human Limbs.—Anecdote of Dr. Nesbit.—Fouché.—Death an eternal Sleep.—The Mob, the most fearful of all Governments.

THE sail down the Saone from Chalons is a very pleasant one. The banks of the river have a quiet beauty; towns are frequent; magnificent bridges frequently span its current; you catch occasional views of the Alps; and, as you approach Lyons, its waters are pressed into a narrow channel, rocks rise on either hand, you shoot through a narrow gorge, pass under the hills of Fauvières and Sainte Foi, and are soon landed upon the quays of the "City of Silks." The approach to it by the Saone is very fine—"magnificent," was the exclamation of one of our party. We put up at the Hotel l'Univers, where we care not to lodge again until the fare is a little more in keeping with the charges. They sustain to each other an inverse ratio.

This greatest silk factory of the world, and the second city of France, is on the tongue of land formed by the junction of the Saone and the Rhone, and on the precise spot where soil, fuel, climate, water, and facility of communication furnish the elements of a great city. Both rivers are spanned by bridges of the most solid masonry. The city is crowded—dirty; and its narrow streets, paved with small stones, are often very offensive. The rivers and mountains hem in the population ; and the streets, in some places, rise so perpendicularly against the hills as to seem like ladders. There are some fine squares, one of which, Bellecour, with a statue of Louis XIV., is said to be one of the grandest in Europe. It did not so impress us.

It was not the noble warehouses that line the rivers, nor its world-famed factories, but its histories, that deeply interested me. Lyons was the Lugdunum of the Romans, and was the scene of the great labors of the Christian Irenæus. It was the scene of a fearful persecution against the Christians under Marcus Aurelius, who were here murdered until men became weary of bloodshed. Their murdered bodies were burned, and their ashes cast into the rivers, that there might be nothing of them left to disgrace the world ! This was the residence of Peter de Vaud, that eminent confessor of the Middle Ages, who gave his name to the Waldensian Christians, who from the days of the apostles have kept the pure light of truth burning in the valleys of the Alps. This was a scene of vast suffering during the religious wars of the sixteenth century, when, in the murder and banishment of the Huguenots, France cast from her bosom the purifying salt. Since then, morally, it has been a festering mass of corruption. But the revolutionary scenes which were here enacted reached the very sublime of cruelty.

The citizens, in self-preservation, arrayed themselves in opposition to the Terrorists of Paris—Robespierre, Danton, and Marat. Under the command of Precy, they made a most determined resistance, and endured an awful siege. After the most heroic acts and endurance, Precy fled, and Couthon entered the city at the head of the army of the Convention. And soon there commenced a scene of cold, ruthless carnage, from which the mind and heart shrink with horror. Collot d'Herbois, a low actor who was hissed from the stage, and whose vanity was turned into ferocity by the insult—Fouché, who gave up the pursuit of the priesthood for turmoil and intrigue—and Dorfeuille, became the leaders of the Jacobins. Every body, man, woman, and child, suspected of royal leanings, or of sympathy with Precy, was placed on the proscribed list. The city was given up to demolition. Prisons were crowded. A permanent scaffold was erected in front of the town hall, where executions were continued for ninety days without interruption. Sand was scattered on the streams of human blood every evening, which, by the constant trampling of the people, thirsting to see their fellow-citizens die, became a red and fetid mud, which soon covered the square and reeked in the air! When this could not be longer endured, the scaffold was placed over a sewer, into which the streaming blood ran, and was carried into the Rhone. And when the executions increased, like the pulsations of an inflamed body, the scaffold was placed in the centre of the Pont Morand, over the river. The flowing blood was swept into the river, and the headless bodies and bodiless heads were cast over the parapets of the bridge into the "arrowy Rhone!" The very washerwomen had to move up the stream to prevent their clothes from being stained. The victims were generally the young men of the city and surrounding country, whose age was their crime.

But even this wholesale butchery was not sufficiently rapid to gratify the thirst of the Jacobins for the blood of "the aristocrats." They were tied together in companies, led across the bridge into the low lands on the opposite banks of the Rhone, placed in a straight line, and then mowed down by cannon! The mangled bodies of men were hung upon the trees which surround the square Bellecour, and festoons of limbs were extended from tree to tree all around, for the purpose of teaching the people the power and the vengeance of the Convention, of which Robespierre was now the head.

And there I was, walking over the square once covered with that red and fetid mud, and under the trees once festooned with human limbs, and standing on the bridge where the guillotine did such fearful execution, and looking over upon the low plain of the Brotteaux, where those scenes of horror were enacted—men placed in rows before the devouring cannon! It was here the anger of the Revolution rose up to the power of a divine scourge.

After a recital like this, no person will find fault with the following anecdote told of Dr. Nesbit, as famous for his keen and ready wit as for his profound scholarship. He was at a dinner-party in Philadelphia during the progress of the French Revolution, when the recently received news from Europe was the engrossing topic of conversation. Several politicians of the Jefferson school were there, strong in their sympathies with French Republicanism. The Doctor was silent for some time. On being asked his opinion, he gave it thus: "I had," said he, in his broad Scotch accent, "a queer dream last night. I dreamed I died, and went to hell. I went to the door and knocked, but nobody came to open it. I knocked again and again, but nobody came. After knocking a good while, the old de'il himself came to the door and asked what I wanted. I told him I wanted to enter hell. Go your way, said the old fellow, slamming the door in my face, I can not let you in; I have nobody to take care of you, for all the other de'ils are gone to help carry on the French Revolution."

Surely it would seem as if such men as D'Herbois, Fouché, Dorfeuille, Robespierre, Danton, Chalier, Dubois-Crancé, so utterly destitute of all feelings of humanity, so utterly demoniacal in disposition, so cool in their cruelties, must have been natives of Pandemonium. Impiety with them was patriotism; cruelty was love of liberty; their love for the poor they showed by the murder of the rich, and proclaimed that the French people recognized no law or authority but those of their sovereignty and omnipotence! It was the human butcher Fouché, according to Lamartine, who ordered a figure of Sleep to be placed over the gates of the cemeteries, with this inscription: "*Death is an eternal sleep.*" Surely, in his case, the desire must have been the father of the thought, for who would not prefer annihilation to a resurrection with the blood of murdered thousands clamoring for vengeance, and to the scrutiny of an unerring and omnipotent Judge, who will by no means clear the guilty!

What scenes of fearful violence have been perpetrated on our globe! There is no safety for the right, the true, the good, but in the maintenance of law and order. If these can be maintained with free institutions, well; if not, let them be maintained with whatever institutions. A bad king is a bad thing; but a ruthless mob, with no reason but passion; yielding to the advice of the most violent; bent only to gratify its prejudices; loud as the thunder and blind as the tornado—this is the worst thing earth knows. The plagues of the Middle Ages were angels' visits in comparison with it.

CHAPTER XVI.

Lyons.—Down the Rhine: its Scenery.—Nuns: their Appearance.—An Inference.—A Contrast.—A startling Incident.—Avignon.—Split in the Popedom: its Causes.—The Popes of Avignon: their Palace.—The butcher Jourdan.—The Cathedral.—The Tarpæan Rock.—The Inquisition.—The Museum.—Old Mortality.—A Conversation with Mine Host.—Petrarch and Laura.

We left Lyons without any regrets for Avignon. The city, as you depart from it, looks, as when approaching it, very fine. Many houses appeared as if they were hung up on the sides of the hills. We thought of the crimsoned waters that once filled the channel, and of the mutilated bodies floating on the waves, lodging on the sand-banks, caught in the shrubbery, and putrefying in the sun! But that fearful reign of terror was ended, may it not be hoped, never to return? But who knows what to hope or fear from France? Wielding great power, with a fickle, imaginative, impulsive, irreligious, unprincipled people, there is much to hope, there is more to fear.

The steamers on the lower Rhone are very long and very narrow. In this thing they are strikingly peculiar. They draw but little water; their accommodations are very poor. The river is rapid, but shallow. The country is broken into mountains and sharp rocks; and here and there you catch a view of snowy mountain peaks which hide their heads in the clouds. On either bank there is a rapid succession of villages, which seem very dirty and uncomfortable, and some very picturesque residences. On the summit of the hills, and cut into the solid rocks, are seen ruins of castles and fortresses erected by the barons and feudal lords of the Middle Ages, and old walls and foundations which date back to the days of Julius Cæsar, to whom this river was very familiar. It would seem impossible to build any structure upon points where some of these huge ruins are tottering. Some panoramic views occasionally present themselves of surpassing beauty. The noble bridges form quite an item in the ever-changing scenery, which astonish an American by their frequency, strength, dimensions, and tastefulness.

We had as fellow-passengers several nuns. To those of us from America, they were objects of some curiosity. The prima donna wore a large crucifix, and moved with an air of authority. She was large, coarse in features, clumsy in her walk, and looked neither like Lent nor Good Friday. To my certain knowledge, on the day of our travel she abstained not from meat or wine. Her companions were like her. All the *pictures* I have seen of nuns represent them as very pretty, but all the nuns I have ever seen were the reverse; and my inference is, that voluntary nuns are those whose convictions are deepened by every look they take in the mirror, that they have but few hopes of matrimony. They chatted a good deal together; they were by no means so rapt in meditations on the Virgin as not to observe every thing passing around them. They looked at me as if they suspected heresy. At a certain hour in the afternoon I found them together reading a missal, and by their side a fine Frenchwoman, of delicately chiseled form and fine face, reading a New Testament. I could not help regarding them as representatives of the two systems of Protestantism and Popery.

There are boats anchored on the Rhone and fastened to the banks, which rise and fall with the water, for the debarking and embarking of passengers. As we were approaching one of them, a wild scream rose from its deck. A Frenchman who had enlisted for Africa, and who, with knapsack on his back, was waiting to come on board, fell into the stream. It was there deep and very rapid. I saw him for a minute or two, with head above the current, but he sank to rise no more! The boat remained a few minutes longer on account of the accident, and then we were away as if nothing had happened! His traveling companion came on board, who showed his feelings of sorrow by soon falling asleep. O, how little are men impressed by the passage of an immortal soul into eternity!

We left Lyons at six in the morning, and at a little after five in the afternoon, we were landed at Avignon, under the shadow of the towering cliff which overhangs the Rhone. We went to the Hotel l'Europe, one of the most neat, pleasant, and agreeable houses we met in all our travels.

The history of Avignon gives it an interest it could not otherwise possess. Its streets are narrow, crooked, and unclean; and it presents every where the evidence of decline. During the terrible split in the Church which boasts of its unity, seven popes reigned here from 1305 to 1377. Two great families arose in the bosom of Italy, the Guelphs and the Ghibellines, whose interests came into collision. The family quarrel extended through the state, and through the kingdoms of Continental Europe, and through the Church. Princes, people, and kingdoms, as they sided with this family or that, took their names. The family quarrel became, in time, a contest for principles; and the wars of the Guelphs and the Ghibellines became the struggle between the spiritual and temporal power, through which it was necessary for Western Europe to pass in order to break the power of the Pope, which was crushing all national independence. In this quarrel we find the causes of the split in the popedom.

By the bribery and intrigue of Philip the Fair, an ambitious and mercenary man, De Got, was elected Pope, who took the name of Clement V., and, to keep away from the influence of the Italian cardinals, fixed his residence in Avignon, which had been subject to the Popes since the Albigensian wars. After the death of De Got, there were awful quarrels among the cardinals as to a successor. They finally agreed to elect any one that De Ossa, bishop of Porto, would nominate. He, kind fellow, nominated himself, and he was installed in Avignon as John XXII. He was succeeded by Benedict XII., a weak man, whose tomb is shown you in the old Cathedral. To him succeeded two or three other men, famed for nothing but wickedness and duplicity, until fear of marauders induced Gregory XI. to remove his court to Rome in order to secure protection. This residence of the papal court in Avignon is called by popish writers "*the Babylonish captivity of the Popes.*" What a blessing to the world if, like the ten tribes, they had been lost forever!

And there upon the top of the rock, called De Dons stands the old palace of the popes, a Gothic building, with high, thick walls, and narrow windows, which might serve for a palace, prison, or fortification. It is now a prison and a barrack, guarded by French soldiery from all entrance by strangers. It was here the human butcher, Jourdan, perpetrated his fearful murders on men, women, and children.

And there, too, is the old Cathedral by its side, where popes said mass, and then retired to intrigue in the affairs of kings and nations. We saw a part of a mass performed there, and heard, for a few minutes, a lazy-looking priest harangue some old women from a pulpit. He seemed earnest, and they sleepy. And by the old palace stands a lofty tower upward of two hundred feet high, from which persons were cast down, for summary death, during the frenzy of the Revolution. It is the Tarpæan rock of Avignon. The stains made by the blood of the murdered are yet pointed out to you by the guide. And in going down to the town, you are led through dark arched ways, with gratings and dungeons on either hand, which once belonged to that "godly and pious institution," the Inquisition. O, if those gratings and dungeons could speak!

There is here an old museum filled with curiosities, and having many fine paintings; some from the pencils of the Vernets, father, son, and grandson. We saw there an old man copying inscriptions from the stones, who seemed as old as the stones themselves, and not unlike them in color. He looked as if disentombed with them. He was certainly the Old Mortality of Avignon.

"And where do you go, Monsieur?" said my polite host to me, on paying my bill, and as I ordered my baggage, and in quite Anglified French.

"To Rome, sir," I replied.

"Be you a Catholique?" he again asked.

"No," I replied, affecting some surprise, "I am a Protestant; there are not many Catholics in America, save those who go there from Europe. The religion of Popery does not suit our institutions."

With a peculiar shrug of the shoulder, and a peculiar accent, which left you in doubt whether he spoke in fun or in faith, he replied, "You do not understand the religion Catholique in Amerique. It suits itself to all the institutions in the vorld." But America and the world is beginning to understand the "religion Catholique," and to regard it as it deserves.

As this was the residence of Petrarch, and the birthplace of Laura, we made some inquiries about them; but their names were unknown to those of whom we made inquiry, and we had no time to seek those better informed.

CHAPTER XVII.

Avignon to Marseilles.—Mixed People.—The City.—The Sea.—Polite Captain.—Marseillaise Hymn: its History.—Dietrick's Fate.—De Lisle.—Pensioned by Louis Philippe.—The Hymn itself.

THE ride by railway from Avignon to Marseilles is a very pleasant one. The country is mostly level around you, with occasionally broken hills and shaggy rocks, and glimpses now and then of mountains towering in the distance. Its historical associations have much to interest the antiquarian and the Protestant. The longest tunnel we ever saw is on this route, said to be four miles through a solid rock. While passing through it, the cars were lighted by a lamp in their roof. Within about twenty miles of Marseilles, we came on a little spot of surpassing beauty, in form like a large wash-basin, containing one or two hundred acres; and from the bottom to the top it was richly and beautifully cultivated. The ways of admission to it were tunneled through its guardian rocks. To catch the sea breeze, you had only to ascend to the top of the basin; to bask in a summer's sun, and to breathe the air of Southern France perfumed with flowers, you had only to descend to its bottom. A more beautiful spot I never beheld; and yet, as if there can be no Eden without a serpent, it was marred by women performing field-labor, and driving about mules and asses. In about three hours from the time we left Avignon, we were put down at Marseilles, an old sea-port town, and the great depôt of France on the Mediterranean.

Here we found ourselves at once in a new climate and among a mixed people. French, English, Jews, Turks, Arabs, we met every where. The Frank, with his unvarying mustache; the Jew, with his long beard; the Turk, with his turban; the Arab, with his bishop's sleeves on his thighs, were to us objects of curiosity. Here we expected to meet a party from which we separated in Paris, but they had left for us a note, and passed on. We soon found ourselves, to our sorrow, in the hands of a "commissionaire," a kind of waiter to be met at the principal hotels, to accommodate and to fleece strangers. Against these horse-leeches, every where, from London, all the way round again to London, I would warn every traveler. When I go abroad again, I will be my own "commissionaire."

Though a very old city, Marseilles has but few objects of interest. It was founded six hundred years before Christ. It early became an ally of Rome. Having espoused the side of Pompey, it was besieged and taken by Cæsar. Subsequently it became famous for its commerce, its fine sailors, and for its schools of learning. In the opinion of Cicero, it was "*the Athens of Gaul.*"

It was here we had our first view of the Mediterranean Sea, so associated with all my recollections of early classical studies. And when we trod the deck of the steamer Bosphore, as she was plowing her way to Naples, we thought of the fleets of Agamemnon, of Ulysses, and of the dangers of Æneas, and of Paul, upon the same waves! The weather was very fine, and the sea seemed as blue and placid as if made of molten glass.

My friend and myself were the only persons speaking English on board, and we had the fine cabin to ourselves. Our little French was put to a severe test; and when laughing at our blunders, in the way of apology, I would sometimes say to the captain, "Je parle la langue Française très mauvais." And, without a smile, he would reply with energy and emphasis, "Très bien, très bien, monsieur." An Englishman will smile at your mistakes, and sometimes ridicule you because of them; a Frenchman, never. But he is often polite at the expense of his sincerity. And the not-understanding look of the captain, as we asked him some questions, and his "non comprendre, monsieur," at the close, formed a contrast with his "très bien, monsieur," broad enough even to prove to him that he flattered our French beyond its merits. Beyond a certain point, flattery becomes fun, if not falsehood. So I must regard all flattery of my French until I understand it better.

The "Marseillaise Hymn" was associated in my mind with the city of Marseilles, and, supposing it was written there, I made some inquiry in reference to it. As a national song, it had prodigious influence during the Revolution; and so often has it been sung, with joy, by Terrorists, Jacobins, and Revolutionists, and heard with paleness and trembling by the friends of monarchy and legitimacy, that it is engraved on the very soul of France. Its awful chorus,

> "Aux armes, citoyens! formez vos battaillons!
> Marchons! qu'un sang impur abreuve nos sillons!"

has often caused the blood of the man in blouse to boil

over, and that of the aristocrat to freeze. Its history is in this wise:

Early in the Revolution, Rouget de Lisle, a native of the Jura Mountains, was a young officer of the garrison at Strasburg. He was a musician, a poet, a soldier. He was often an inmate there of the family of one Dietrick, with whose daughters he became a favorite. The family was poor but patriotic. "I have one bottle of wine left," said Dietrick one evening to his daughters: "bring it, and we will drink to liberty and our country. Our city is going to have a patriotic ceremony, and De Lisle must compose a hymn for the occasion." The bottle was brought and exhausted. De Lisle retired at midnight, his whole soul inflamed. He spent the night humming and rhyming, rhyming and humming. He dozed. Rising with the day, he wrote the hymn and the tune. He called the family of Dietrick together, and a few other friends. They were all musicians, and loved poetry. They sang, they wept, they rejoiced together. The national song of France was written. It flew from club to club, from city to city. It was sung at the opening of all the clubs of Marseilles. A band of young men, called "the Confederates of Marseilles," marched to Paris to aid the conspirators there. These confederates received the name of Marseillaise; and, singing the hymn as they went, it spread over France like lightning. Hence its name, "the Marseillaise Hymn." The language and the tune are peculiarly exciting, and, when sung in full chorus, is said to inspirit even a horse for the battle. Its singing was forbidden by the Bourbons, but in the revolution of 1830 it became again the national song.

But the history of this famous hymn is not ended. Dietrick, whose wine and exhortation inspired the poet to write it, was marched to the scaffold, to the sound of the notes first sung in his own house by the aid of his family and a few friends! Nor is this all. The author himself was proscribed, and fled. In passing along the wild gorges of the Alps, he heard its wild notes rising around him, and he shuddered. "What do they call that hymn?" he asked the guide. "The Marseillaise," was the reply. He himself called it "An offering to Liberty." It was thus he first knew the name under which his hymn was destined to immortality. It is right to add that Louis Philippe, on ascending the throne of France, found out Rouget de Lisle, who was then seventy years old, and granted him a pension of 1500 francs from his own private purse.

This digression will be forgiven by those who have any true conception of the hymn and its influence. It is caused by the power of association, the name of the city suggesting the national song. It may induce some reader to cultivate an acquaintance with perhaps the most exciting and soul-stirring national anthem ever written. We know of no good English translation of it, and we give the hymn as corrected by Lamartine.

THE MARSEILLAISE.

I.

Allons, enfants de la patrie,
Le jour de gloire est arrivé!
Contre nous, de la tyrannie
L'étendart sanglant est levé.
Entendez vous dans ces campagnes
Mugir ces féroces soldats!

Ils viennent jusque dans vos bras
Egorger vos fils et vos compagnes !
Aux armes, citoyens ! formez vos bataillons !
Marchons ! qu'un sang impur abreuve nos sillons !

II.

Que veut cette horde d'esclaves,
De traîtres, de rois conjurés ?
Pour qui ces ignobles entraves
Ces fers dès longtemps préparés ?
Français, pour vous, ah ! quel outrage,
Quels transports il doit exciter !
C'est vous qu'on ose méditer
De rendre à l'antique esclavage ;
Aux armes, &c.

III.

Quoi ! ces cohortes étrangères
Feraient la loi dans nos foyers ?
Quoi ! ces phalanges mercenaires
Terrasseraient nos pères guerriers ?
Grand Dieu ! par des mains enchainées,
Nos fronts sous le joug se ploieraient ;
De vils despotes deviendraient
Les maîtres de nos destineés !
Aux armes, &c.

IV.

Tremblez, tyrans ! et vous, perfides,
L'opprobre de tous les partis !
Tremblez, vos projets parricides
Vont enfin recevoir leur prix !
Tout est soldat pour vous combattre :
S'ils tombent nos jeunes héros,
La France en produit les nouveaux,
Contre vous tout prêts à se battre.
Aux armes, &c.

V.

Français, en guerriers magnanimes
Portez ou retenez vos coups ;
Epargnes ces tristes victimes
A regret s'armant contre vous.

Mais ces despotes sanguinaires,
Mais les complices de Bouillé,
Tous ces tigres sans pitié
Déchirent le sein de leur mère.
Aux armes, &c.

VI.

Amour sacré de la patrie,
Conduis, soutiens nos bras vengeurs!
Liberté, liberté chérie,
Combats avec tes défenseurs!
Sous nos drapeaux que la Victoire
Accoure à tes mâles accents;
Que tes ennemis expirants
Voient ton triomphe et notre gloire!
Aux armes, &c.

VERSE SUNG BY CHILDREN.

Nous entrerons dans la carrière,
Quand nos aînés n'y seront plus;
Nous y trouverons leur poussière
Et la trace de leurs vertus!
Bien moins jaloux de leur survivre
Que de partager leur cercueil,
Nous aurons le sublime orgueil
De les venger ou de les suivre!
Aux armes, &c.

CHAPTER XVIII.

Sail to Leghorn.—A Day in its Bay.—Robbing by Passports.—Leghorn from the Sea.—Corsica.—Napoleon.—A great Man a great Need.—Civita Vecchia: its Fortress.—Placard on Nôtre Dame.—Civita Vecchia from the Sea.—Ostia.—Bay of Naples.—Landing in Italy.

OUR sail down the Mediterranean was remarkably pleasant. The sea was as quiet to Leghorn as an inland lake on a calm, bright summer's day. Until midnight we gazed upon the heavens above us, studded with stars, which were reflected from the glassy bosom of the sea, and with imaginations filled with dreamy thoughts of the scenes which a thousand ages since had transpired on these waters, we went to our stateroom. We awoke in Livornia, as the French call Leghorn.

After looking around us, and knowing our circumstances, we needed no valet to inform us that we were in Italy. A strong fortress on our right was guarded by Austrian soldiers in white or wool-colored blouse. Our passports, given to our captain at Marseilles, were sent ashore to get for us permission to land, but no permission came. We wished simply to land to see the city; but there was no landing without paying a bribe to the police. Every thing in Italy goes by "bribery and corruption." We declined the bargain, and were, in consequence, confined to the deck of our steamer all day, gazing upon boats, ships, soldiers, sailors, priests, Jews, Arabs, and Frenchmen, scolding and jabbering all around us. The extortion hitherto practiced on us was endurable, but in Italy it became insufferable from its intensity and frequency, and this mainly through the system of passports. Consuls, captains, keepers of hotels, porters, commissionaires, waiters, custom and police officers, are united in a great conspiracy to plunder travelers. Consuls, against law and instruction, charge for signing your passport, and on entering and leaving the city it has to be re-signed and repaid. You can not turn round without paying for the privilege. If you enter a church or museum, a person demands your cane or umbrella, and you have to pay for their release. You are followed every where by the most perfect system of annoyance, and for the purpose of getting your money. The system of passports was designed to catch rogues, and to prevent the going at large of political disturbers of the peace of tyrants, but it is retained for the purpose of robbing honest travelers. It is the burden of complaint every where and by every body, and Britain and America should interfere to break it up. The nearer you get to the seat of the Pope, the more you are "out of humanity's reach."

A little bustle, and our boat was to sea again for Civita Vecchia. From the bay of Leghorn we had a good view of the city and surrounding country. The city is directly on the sea, and presents nothing inviting. The hills surrounding it are dotted with houses unsheltered by trees. But few houses and no trees are to be seen in the country; hence it presents from the sea a very dreary and barren aspect. On our way down we passed the islands of Corsica and Elba, whose only interest is their connection with Napoleon Bonaparte—the one as the place of his birth, and the other of his confinement for a few months. They are within sight of one another and of Italy. That great man has impressed his character upon Europe. You meet with the traces of his power and genius every where. O, for another such man, with all his genius and more than his morals. What Europe now wants is a great man. A man uniting in himself the genius of Napoleon and the virtue of Washington, would be Heaven's greatest gift at this hour to Continental Europe. Before such a man the demon of despotism would fall prostrate; petty and priestly tyrants would flee away; the hearts of all desponding patriots would be filled with hope and joy; there would be a universal rising of all those sighing in silence over their mental and moral slavery; and free institutions would rise like magic, from the North Cape to the Mediterranean, and from the Straits of Dover to the Sea of Azof. The whole earth should cry to heaven for such a man!

We awoke in the morning at the sea-port of Rome, Civita Vecchia, and within the temporal dominions of the Pope! The stern towers were frowning around us in our very narrow harbor, and the third and fourth stories of white brick houses were looking over the fortifications upon us. French soldiers were in all the fortresses, and the Papal flag floated from all their summits. Churches and crosses seemed numerous—the ringing of mass and convent bells was incessant. One of the fortifications bore the inscription that it was erected by Pope Alexander VII., another by Pius VII., while yet another bore the coat of arms of the Pope, in heavy bass-relief. What inscriptions on towers and bulwarks by those pretending to be the vicars of Jesus Christ, who came to bring good tidings of great joy to all people! Is it not a wonder the priests themselves do not see the baseness of their impositions upon the credulity of the ignorant, and for very shame abandon them! No wonder that these shaven-pated sinners were horror-struck on learning that a placard was placed one night on the door of Nôtre Dame at Paris, the object of which was to contrast Christ and the Pope as shepherds. It was to this amount:

"Christ gave his life for the sheep,
The Pope takes the life of the sheep."

Looking back upon Civita Vecchia from the deck of our steamer as we departed for Naples, it looks as insignificant as it is. There are small hills in the background surmounted by stunted pines, but the whole face of the country looks as barren as Popery can make it. Every thing seems smitten with death or disease. No houses—no tillage—no flocks or lowing herds—no trees, fences, or vineyards. The country was once settled; and why not now? Late in the afternoon old Ostia came to view. We were near enough to see its few houses, but not a sail, nor a boat of any kind or description was there to indicate the mouth of the Tiber! O, what a change from the time when the richest argosies sought its channel, to deposit their richest cargoes of treasures in the lap of her who sat proudly on the seven hills as mistress of the world! "And is that Ostia?" said I, with an air of surprise, to our captain. "Oui, Monsieur," he replied, with such a toss of both his shoulders as seemed for a moment to bury his head between them.

After spending a third night upon the waters of the Mediterranean, we awoke in the morning in the thrice beautiful Bay of Naples. The heavy splash of the anchor in the waters broke our slumbers. I raised myself in my berth, and opened the window of my stateroom to see where I was, and what was the matter, and lo! the very first object that arrested my eye was the smoking summit of the fiery Vesuvius! The desire indulged from the hour I first read of a volcano was now gratified, and there before me, belching forth volumes of smoke, stood, although one of the smallest, yet one of the most famous of them all! The emotions it excited within me I can not describe.

The boats to carry us and our baggage to the Custom-house were soon in waiting for us. As we descended the ladder, a voice from below asked, "Is there any body here for the Hotel New York?" The name of the hotel, and a man speaking English, attracted our attention; we took him for our guide. We landed, and here first touched Italian soil. Every thing seemed new, strange, peculiar. Such hosts of beggars sunning themselves by the water's side, and so ragged and filthy! Such crowds of soldiers meeting us every where, at every corner! Such swarms of priests tripping along in three-cornered hats and long dresses, pinned up at one side so as to facilitate their walking! Such swarms of donkeys, laden with commodities often twice their own size, and a driver sitting on the top to boot! Every thing was new, and many surprising. With very little trouble we passed the Custom-house, and were soon pleasantly lodged in a room facing the magnificent bay, and from which, day and night, we could look out upon one of the most beautiful panoramic views in the world, one of whose attractive objects is the perpetually smoking Vesuvius.

CHAPTER XIX.

Naples.—Carthusian Monks.—The entire View.—Vesuvius.—Herculaneum.—Pompeii.—Cemetery.—The Morals of the People.—Naples thoroughly Popish.—Its Beggars.—Its Priests.—Its Ignorance.—Its Superstitions.—Its Wickedness.—Its awful Despotism.—Ferdinand the "Model King."—The blessings of Popery.

THERE is an old saying among the Neapolitans, "see Naples and die." It is certainly a city beautiful for situation. The bay is a deep crescent, and the city, in horse-shoe form, rises all around it. As you are rowed to the place of landing, the hill on which frowns the Castle of St. Elmo rises before you; on one heel of the horse-shoe stands the smoking Vesuvius, on the other a headland crowded with houses, and famous for the perhaps fabled tomb of Virgil. And the city itself is mainly built on the declivity of a mountain, rising from the water in the form of an amphitheatre to its summit. The very summit is crowned with the Castle, strongly fortified. And just beneath it is a capacious convent, from whose windows, porches, and walls may be taken the most enchanting views of the city, the bay, the islands, the fiery mountain, and of every thing which has given the Bay of Naples the pre-eminence for beauty. This is the Carthusian monastery of S. Martino, whose inmates, it is said, but rarely speak—thus doing penance for the sin of having tongues! Although famed in history for its many and terrible rebellions, and now for the ferocity and brutality of its princely and priestly despotism, it bears the name of *fidelissima;* but this describes, not its moral characteristics, but its beautiful situation, its fertile soil, its balmy atmosphere, its clear blue sky, and its other manifold physical blessings. Indeed, as you breathe its mild air, and gaze upon its splendid scenery, as you slowly run your eye along the splendid panorama, from Vesuvius on the right, over Capri and Ischia, to Pausilippo on the left, you soon feel a heart beating within you with pulsation so generous, as to induce you to forgive the lazy Neapolitan who would insist that "Naples is a piece of heaven fallen down to earth."

Naples, its points of beauty, its surrounding curiosities, its famed antiquities, have been very often described. As seen from the shore, Vesuvius, with its twin mountain, seems like two eggs of immense size, joined from centre to bottom, but separated at the top—the one an extinguished, the other a smoking volcano. Herculaneum is between the mountain and the city, yet buried under the lava which is congealed there into a solid rock, hard as flint. You enter it by a rough descent, with lighted torches. Pompeii, on the other side of the volcano, and about fourteen miles from Naples, was buried in cinders and ashes, which are easily removed. It is uncovered, and looks somewhat as would have done "the burnt district" of New York, after the fire of 1835, if the walls had been left standing up to the first or second story, and the rubbish all removed. You walk along its open streets, under a burning sun, with nothing to fear but lizards, which are jumping and crawling around you in myriads. Its history, but nothing else, is intensely interesting. The

Amphitheatre, where gladiators fought with wild beasts, with its seats of marble, sufficient to accommodate thousands, rising one above another, is a noble ruin, and in fine preservation. The Cemetery of Naples, of which but few travelers have taken notice, is a place of great beauty, far surpassing that of Père la Chaise. In its centre is a vast under-ground room, over which extends an open yard, with many trap-doors in it, into which the poor dead are cast, with or without clothes, as they may have any or none ; but the tombs of the rich are often superb. Shelves for coffins, eight or ten high, are made in walls of solid masonry. These shelves are closed on the interment of a body. Some large chapels are filled in this way, the walls around being crowded with the dead, and covered with inscriptions from floor to ceiling.

But that which had for us most interest was the moral state of the people. Here, perhaps, of all other places in Christendom, has Popery all things to its mind. The king and queen are intensely popish. It was to the protection of the Neapolitan king the Pope fled from Rome. The security which Pio Nono could not find in Rome or the Vatican, he found at Gaeta and in the palace of Portici, under the shadow of Vesuvius. Here he was worshiped as the vicegerent of heaven, when he was regarded on the Tiber as a tyrant.

And the priests have every thing to their desire in Naples. The king, queen, government—the systems of religious instruction and of education, are entirely in their hands. And so it has been for ages. Naples, with all its institutions, is in the hands of the priests as the clay is in the hands of the potter; and here is the place where, without let or hinderance, Popery has had the grandest opportunity of showing its tendencies and producing its fruits. And what are its influences and fruits, as seen in the religious and moral state of the people?

The moment you place your foot on the quay of Naples, you feel at once that you have landed in a city of beggars. You meet them on landing—they dog you to the custom-house—to your carriage—to your hotel. They meet you in the streets, and, if you give away a few coppers, they swarm around you. You see them in groups upon all the quays, around all the churches, in all the public squares, and in all kinds of mutilation and rags. They sleep in the markets, or on the steps, or in the porches of churches; and in the city of Naples there are said to be thirty thousand and upward of the most beggarly-looking beggars to be seen in the world. And yet every thing you see in the shape or dress of a priest, save the wretched-looking mendicant monks, are clothed in fine black cloth, and fine linen, and silk stockings, and shining shoe-buckles, and look as if they fared sumptuously every day. The priests of Naples are the most sleek, rotund, joyous, well-fed, self-satisfied set of looking men I ever saw. They look and act as if they were in clover. Somehow or other, priests and beggars swarm together. Where is an exception?

Naples is a city of ignorance. There are humane and charitable institutions there, but there is no system of education that has in view the masses. None of those swarming beggars can read. Such is the fact as to the tier of people above the beggars. The merest fraction of the people know how to read. There is a college for the sons of the aristocracy, whose students wear a military uniform; there are schools where, at great expense, the children of the wealthy may be educated. But nothing is done for the instruction of the people. There are neither "godless" nor godly schools there. Hence Naples is an ignorant city. Somehow or other, priests and ignorance are always found together. Where the priests wield the influence, the masses are in ignorance. Where is an exception?

Naples is a wicked city. We collected statistics in proof of this, but we can not here state them. But the evidences of this wickedness you meet every where. So numerous are crosses, Virgins, pictures of Christ, lighted candles, and other papal emblems, and so much external reverence is paid to these things, that a stranger might infer there is much piety there. But when you see men bowing to the Virgin, and swearing at the same time—gambling under a picture of Christ in agony on the cross—drinking, dancing, and carousing in the presence of a box with a glass door containing an image of Mary and Bambino, with a candle burning before it—when you see priests in shovel hats, and monks with ropes around their loins, playing cards in the open streets, what further evidence do you need of a wicked and corrupt city? If the pious and the priests do so, what must be the conduct of the sinful and the common people? And the true state of the case is such as to sustain any inference we may draw. Where the priests wield the influence, the masses of the people are wicked. Where is an exception?

Of the gross superstition of Naples, what can we say?

You see the proof of it every where. You see it in the processions of the Host to the chambers of the dying—in their general processions—in the multiplication of emblems of worship—in the miserable miraculous juggle as to the blood of St. Januarius, a cheat practiced by the priests on the people three or four times a year! I was in the cathedral church of this saint on "St. John's day," which is a high day in Italy. There was high mass going on at the altar, at which three cardinals were serving. A servitor handed his censer to another, and, stepping down from the altar, offered his services. We went to the tomb of the saint under the altar—to the little chapel where the blood liquefies—and as the man in livery explained all with an air more of incredulity than of belief, I could not help muttering *shame! shame!* If priests in America will strive to explain the sentence of the Madiai in Tuscany so as to turn away its sharp point from Popery and its priests, what explanation will they attempt of the cheat as to the blood of St. Januarius? If they say it is a true miracle, the country will be in a broad laugh; if they admit it to be what it is, a most gross imposition, what follows? Priests and gross superstition go together. Where is an exception? Surely not where they have all things to their liking.

Naples is most despotically governed. The king is a despot, and the priests are his tools and his spies. The prisons are filled with prisoners, among whom are the noblest and truest men of the country. The old Bourbon "*lettres de cachet*," in all their terrible and concealed despotism, are revived; and, without charge, trial, or notice, the very salt of the people are torn from their families and confined in the most noisome and deadly dungeons. The awful revelations of Gladstone in his "Two Letters to the Earl of Aberdeen" will not soon be forgotten by the world. The present fearful despot granted a Constitution, then revoked it, and then cast into prison and into felons' graves the persons that formed it, and sustained it by his command. Cardinals and bishops have written political catechisms, and they are taught by the priests in the schools of the kingdom of the Two Sicilies, which teach that all liberally-minded persons are eternally lost; that the people can establish no fundamental laws, as all such laws must flow from the sovereign; that the people, who are made for submission, can impose no laws upon a sovereign; that a sovereign is not bound to keep his oath when he thinks it good to violate it; and that the Pope can absolve, when necessary, from the obligation of an oath, and from the crime of violating it. With a catechism like this, written by cardinals and bishops, taught by the priest in all the schools, and fully believed by a Bourbon prince, we leave it to our readers to infer what must be the freedom enjoyed, or the despotism felt, by the people of Naples. Priests and despotism go together.

And yet, in the view of the Pope and his priests, the King of Naples is the model king, and his kingdom the model kingdom of the world. He is the monarch of the earth whom Pio Nono most delights to honor. Nor is there a model after which the Pope and his priests would more gladly mould our own happy Republic, were it in their power, than the kingdom of Naples. The apologists for the Duke of Tuscany in the case of the Madiai should be the advocates of Ferdinand.

O the blessings, civil, social, and religious, in reserve for our country, when priests are in power here as they are in Naples!

CHAPTER XX.

The Effect of a Feast-day.—San Carlos.—Mixture.—Capua.—Gaeta: its Sights.—The Three Taverns.—First Sight of Rome.—Italy, from Naples to Rome.—The Face of the Country.—The People.—Woman degraded.—Emblems of Superstition every where.—Mass in a Village.—Light at Gaeta.—Contrast.—Glorious Associations.—Door of Hope.

By the recurrence of a feast-day, which was succeeded by the birth-day of the tyrannical king, we were detained in Naples longer than was comfortable. A feast or fast day down here stops all steamers and stages, and nearly all business; even on the wheels of government they put a brake—not so as to the Sabbath-day. Man's days are sacred; the Lord's day is disregarded. This is the action of Popery every where. On the birth-day of the king, the theatre of San Carlos was opened, and the church opposite to it on the square was brilliantly illuminated. The cross by which it is surmounted was in a blaze of light. Thus Popery mixes and mingles the feast, the theatre, the Church—things the most opposite—in the same dish, always paying a preponderating respect to the earthly element. I stood for some time, in the twilight of the evening, near the door of the San Carlos, to catch a glimpse of royalty and to see the fashion of the city. But the royal family was afraid to risk itself amid the gatherings of a theatre, and the great majority of the men I saw enter were priests and soldiers. The men in shovel-hats looked as if they cared much for the things of this life, and not much for the things of the life which is to come.

When the feast and natal day were over, and conveyances were permitted again to move, we left Naples amid a crowd of boys, priests, and beggars. We soon entered the country, which is finely cultivated. Soon we thundered through the gates of Capua, where Hannibal took up his residence after his great victory at Cannæ, and amid dirty lanes and all kinds of noises, drew up before the Hôtel de Ville. It was any thing but attractive. Who would ever think of Hannibal in connection with such a place! Thence we passed along the valley of the Voltorno—magnificently cultivated and wonderfully productive—to Gaeta, rendered somewhat noted by the hegira of his Holiness a few years since. This place received its name from its being the burial-place of the nurse of Æneas, according to Virgil, and in its immediate vicinity Cicero was put to death by order of Antony. The Mola di Gaeta is beautifully situated on the sea, as is also the town, from which it is separated by a valley. But the town itself is in the broadest contrast with its magnificent situation. Its streets are very narrow, very dirty, and the hotel in which we dined was in every respect like them. The women wore a most peculiar dress, and the shorts of the men reached almost half way to their knees. The women sat in groups in the doors and under the shade of the walls, nursing their children, and picking each other's heads. The oranges were falling from the trees as we rode along, and as we knew that they were clean when skinned, we ate many of them. Thence we passed to Terracina, on the southern extremity of the Pontine Marshes, on the Appian Way, and where once stood, proudly and beautifully, the palace of Galba. After crossing the marshes, we spent an hour or more at a miserable village, the Three Taverns, rendered famous by the visit of Paul. Thence we passed through a beautiful and often broken country until we reached the heights of Frescati, when Rome, reposing at the bottom of the immense basin which here opens upon you, presented itself to view. "Voici la Rome!" exclaimed our French companions. Soon we appeared before the gate Porta Giovanni. After due search and inquiry, we entered the Eternal City; guarded by an officer, we were conducted to the place of customs, and after a thorough search for articles contraband and heretical, we were permitted to file off, each to the hotel of his choice. Very soon I found quiet quarters, after a most dusty and fatiguing ride, in the Hôtel d'Angleterre. I was now in the very heart of the city of Rome!

This ride from Naples to the Tiber, though tiresome, occupying nearly two days and a night, is a very fine one. It gives you new views of Italy, which is much broken, very fertile, presenting beautiful sights, and crowded with a most stupid and debased-looking peasantry. In fertility it seemed to surpass England or France, and you meet every where with groves of oranges and lemons. The fig and the prune abound, and the vine trained from tree to tree, and so trimmed as not to exclude the sun from the culture beneath, forming a sort of net-work twelve or fifteen feet high, gives a fairy aspect to the scenery. Looking simply at its surface, fertility, and climate, Italy is a splendid country.

But the people seem remarkably poor and debased. Women are seen working with men in the fields, and at all kinds of labor, without covering on head or foot, and often not decently clad. We met them often riding asses as do men, and merrily singing with them as they were returning from the fields to their villages in the evening. The villages wear a very faded appearance, and beggars every where assail you. The country is beautiful, the air is balmy, the sky is clear as glass; but you exclaim with amazement as you gaze upon the people, Are these the descendants of the Romans, whose eagles flapped their wings in the triumphs of victory at the extremes of the world?

And the emblems of Popery meet you every where. The pictures of Mary you see in the shops of the butcher, the baker, the shoemaker, and in the gin-shop, over the bottles of wine and brandy. Little alcoves are made for them in the walls by the highways, where they are often placed with candles burning before them. The cross you see every where—in houses, and on them—by the way-side, and in the fields—on the tops of hay-ricks and stacks of grain. And yet there is no scriptural religion among the people. On the Sabbath morning we visited a church in one of the interior villages; a very few people were attending mass, performed by a most clumsy old priest, while a crowded market was going on in the public square, where were priests in dozens, and some of them laughing merrily at the tricks of the mountebanks! So little are people affected by these emblems, multiplied until they become offensive, that we have seen a man at the same time bowing to the Virgin and swearing at his ass! In passing through Gaeta, a woman, spinning flax after the fashion of the place, to save herself in a narrow street, turned into an alcove in the wall in which was an image of the Virgin, which she struck with her flax-stick: she quickly turned round, and, crossing herself, dropped a courtesy. She evidently made the *amende honorable* by asking her pardon! There is no more religion in Italy than when Paganism held dominion there; and there is no more, and probably no less homage to the external symbols of religion than when the people worshiped the *lares* and *penates.* There is no way of addressing an ignorant and brutalized people but through the senses. And as Popery brutalizes the people, it multiplies the objects of sense. Thus did Paganism, and Popery faithfully writes after its copy. This is its true succession.

The American riding through Italy is constantly reminded that he is in a strange land. Convents are seen on the tops of the very highest hills, and you are left to imagine how they are accessible. Nor can you conjecture the reason why they are so located. Villages are very generally built on the slopes of hills, and in positions where they could with ease be very strongly fortified and easily defended. No houses are scattered over the country, as with us—the people, like sheep, go out over the fields by day, and return to the same fold in the evening. When you stop at a village to change horses or to take a meal, the first and last persons you generally see are priests and beggars; and, while equally idle, they differ widely in appearance. The priests are round, sleek, and well-dressed—some of them as fat as Eglon. The common people look as one might suppose the Hebrews looked in Egypt, when, under the cruel tyranny of the Pharaohs, they were obliged to make brick without straw!

And yet you feel that you are treading a soil of hallowed association, whose every road, hill, village, river, mountain, bay, has its stirring history. In this town Hannibal lived. In this narrow pass he was checked by Fabius. Here Cicero lived. There he was killed by the paid assassins of Antony, who cut off his head and hands, and sent them to Rome. Along this road marched the legions of Rome to the conquest of the nations, and on it they marched back again to the Capitol, leading kings captive, with their victorious banners floating over them. In this valley was a death-struggle with Goths and Vandals. On that promontory Paul landed. Here he met the brethren from Rome, and rejoiced with them. Thus every thing has its history, and during every step of your progress you are dreaming of the past and sighing over the present! Paganism ennobled, Popery has degraded Italy. There is no hope for it but in the removal of the priestly tyranny that has ground it to powder. Let Italy exchange the missal for the Bible, the priest for the true minister, the authority of the Pope for that of God, and it may be again among the nations what it has been. This is its only door of hope.

CHAPTER XXI.

Dreams realized.—Rome from the Tower of the Capitoline.—The Tiber.—The Seven Hills.—The Magnificent vanishes.—The Ruins. —Bathos.—The Corso: its Appearance.—Afternoon Walk.—Rome in June.—A Cause for Thankfulness.

I AM now in Rome, of which I have dreamed, read, and thought from youth up, and in reference to which I have always entertained the hope that I should see it before I should die. My dreams and hopes are all fully realized. I am in the very heart of the city of the Cæsars!

As a thirsty traveler rushes to a water-brook, bends down to the stream, and slakes his thirst at the first draught, so we determined to fill our minds and hearts with Rome by a first sight. For this purpose we ascended the Capitoline Hill, passed, with a bare recognition, the colossal statues of Castor and Pollux, and the magnificent equestrian statue of Marcus Aurelius, and clambered up to the Tower of the Capitoline. We felt disposed to turn away from the views presented at the various angles of ascent, until the eye, without obstruction, could sweep the entire panorama. We gained the highest point, and Rome lay at our feet! The city of the Cæsars, all in ruins, lay on one side of the hill; the city of the Popes, with its palaces and churches, on the other. Beyond the walls, deserted and death-like, lay the Campagna, an irregular plain, which of old contained parts of Latium and Etruria, while the horizon was bounded by the blue line of the ocean, Soracte, the Sabine, and Volscian hills. Hope was lost in fruition; the poetry of our feelings passed away like foam upon the waters, and there lay Rome in its ruins, its splendor, and its prose, before us. And, at the risk of being charged with a want of taste, a want of reverence, a want of historic appreciation, and perhaps many other wants, I will give my own views of men and things as I saw them in Rome.

Looking out from the tower of the Capitol, the Tiber flows beneath you, dividing the city into two equal parts. It is a narrow, muddy, winding stream, spanned by four or five bridges—on which not a mast is seen, nor a boat plying, nor a sign of life, save a machine for catching fish, which, turned by the current, is evermore lazily tossing its arms in the air! You are struck with its utter meanness, and exclaim, "Is that the Tiber?"

You ask your valet, after running your eye around in vain search for them, "Where are the Seven Hills?" And he points you to little swellings here and there within the walls, saying, "That is the Aventine, and that is the Palatine, and that is the Cœlian, and that is the Esquiline, and that is the Quirinal, and that is the Viminal, and this upon which you are standing is the Capitoline." And there they lie, all within a circumference far too narrow to bound the plantation of even a moderate Western farmer! And when it is remembered that cities were built upon those hills—that nations contended in the valleys that separate them—that in these valleys, over which an Indian would shoot his arrow, the Etruscans, the Sabines, the Latins contended for empire, how the magnificent takes its departure from all the views we were led to entertain in our youthful days as to the origin of Rome and the Romans! Indeed, while straining our eyes in the direction of the finger of our valet pointing out this hill and that, we made the remark that, were it not for his kind aid, we could not have found out the seven hills even with a search-warrant. And soon the poetry of "the seven hills" was all gone!

And there beneath us are the ruins of the Roman Forum, consisting of falling pillars, tottering walls, and rubbish in piles, giving obvious indications of former magnificence, strength, and extent. And at a little farther remove are the ruins of the Coliseum, grand, historic, and suggestive of scenes and events from which the mind and heart recoil. And, as we subsequently wandered amid its arches, and around and over its walls and seats, we could recall the day when the holy Ignatius was turned into the area—when that area was crowded with matrons, virgins, confessors, and when wild lions, tigers, leopards were let loose upon them, and, amid the plaudits of some eighty thousand spectators, tore them to pieces! And in full view, scattered over the Esquiline and Palatine Hills, and the space between them, are the column of Trajan, the arch of Titus, the palace of the Cæsars, the baths of Titus, the arch of Constantine, and the ruins of temples, mutely eloquent as to the past and present. The columns and arches are noble—the Coliseum is magnificent, worth going to Rome to see—but, in the main, the ruins have nothing save historic interest; and you are soon lost in a wilderness of foundations and dilapidating walls. And when we saw brawny Italians stuffing the palace of the Cæsars with hay to feed the horses of the French—and swarthy women hoeing potatoes and cabbage upon the top of it—and the Forum changed into a cow market—and other things after the same fashion, the reader may judge how suddenly we fell from the poetic region in which we had so long reveled, into the prosaic bathos of roofless walls, crumbling arches, and piles of brick!

And there, too, is the famous Corso, right under your eye, and running straight as an arrow from the base of the Capitoline to the Piazza del Popolo and the Flaminian Gate! This is the great street of Rome, said in the guide books to have been adorned by at least three popes! And as it derives its name from *horse-races* which were introduced there by the pious pope Paul II., every stranger would expect to find it a wide street, adorned with trees, and crowded with palaces! But not a tree is to be seen there. It is as narrow as John Street in New York. The sidewalks are too narrow for two persons to walk arm-in-arm. The houses are very high and very irregular; and the *palaces*, as they are called, because of the heavy iron gratings of the windows, look more like prisons than places of private and aristocratic residence. The middle of the street is the great promenade; and it is quite peculiar to see in the afternoon a dense crowd in the street, dodging in every direction to save themselves from the carriages which are slowly winding their way along, as if to expose the jewelry and gorgeous attire of their occupants to the view of the pilgrims to the city of the Cæsars. O, if the races of Paul II., of blessed memory, could only be renewed there on a fair afternoon in April, what a scene would be witnessed in the famous Corso! And as, with my friend in travel, we first walked down this street to the Piazza del Popolo, where stands the obelisk of Rhamses, which once stood in Heliopolis as a decoration of the Temple of the Sun, the question was often smilingly asked of one another, "Is this the famous Corso?" When this is the Broadway and the Fifth Avenue of Rome, it requires no very vivid imagination to conjecture what the city, as a whole, must be! We were as much disappointed at the Corso as we were at the "Yellow Tiber," or at seeing cabbages growing on the top of the Palace of the Emperors!

There is, no doubt, more life here during the winter, and at the season when the fasts and feasts of the Church call strangers together to witness the buffoonery of the Carnival, and the dramatic performances of Holy Week, when pope, cardinals, prelates, and priests are the actors; but, during the days of our sojourn, it seemed like a deserted city. Those days were in early June, when the strangers had mostly returned north, and when but few, save the citizens, remained. But few were seen at the various points of interest. There were no houses building—no new streets opening—no ships or steamers on the river—no manufactures—no railway cars whistling along. The shops were all small, and mostly for the sale of pictures, cameos, intaglios, and mosaics; and but few to purchase. For a short while in the afternoon the Corso was crowded; but until then, and afterward, it seemed like a city deserted. French soldiers were there—their drums were beating at all hours in some direction; priests were there in any number, and tripping along with a most self-satisfied air at all hours; and beggars, that always follow priests, as does the shadow its shade, were to be met every where. But yet the city seemed deserted. I felt, in kind, the feeling of loneliness which oppressed me in going through the streets of Pompeii. It would seem as if some dreadful miasma was hanging over it, from which as many as could had fled, and of which those who could not flee lived in constant terror. I thanked God a thousand times that I was neither a Roman nor a papist. And these are mercies for which I have to thank him daily.

But I am not yet done with Rome. "Thus endeth the first lesson."

CHAPTER XXII.

Object stated.—Saint Peter's.—From Top to Bottom.—Chat in the Basement.—Its Grandeur and Amplitude.—Statue of St. Peter.—Its Worship disgusting.—Mass there.—A disappointed Confessor.—The Scene of the Rod.—The Sublime and Ridiculous.—The Confessional, or Tomb of St. Peter.—Poor Ives's Emblems of Office.—The Wafer Taken.—A Farce.

As the great object of my visit to Rome was to see for myself the workings of Popery at the very centre of the system, and under the eye of its infallible head, I sought to render every hour of my time, and all my researches, subservient to my one object. My readers will give me credit, at least, for honesty, when I frankly own that I was as much interested to discover the *foul* arts of the priests, as I was to look upon those immortal productions of the *fine* arts, which, together with its ruins, now form the only attractions of Rome, whose power was once supreme in the world.

Of course we went to St. Peter's, the noblest edifice of its kind in the world, and as we gained the point where we had a first view of its towering front, surmounted by the apostles—of its semicircular colonnades adorned with nearly two hundred statues—of the majestic pillar, sent to Rome by Caligula, that rises in the centre of the piazza—of the fountains which send up their snow-white foam, we stood and gazed in mute wonder! Until now, my disappointment almost reached the point of dejection, but now my expectations rose to the point of astonishment. We entered. Our astonishment rose as we went around the magnificent interior. And as we gazed upon the splendid nave—the gigantic pillars—the stupendous dome that swells up nearly five hundred feet, arrayed in beauty to the very apex—the wonderful creations of art that meet the eye at every point, we felt overwhelmed with a sense of the beautiful and the magnificent! We clambered up to the top and looked again over the city, and feasted our eyes upon every thing that could be seen from that elevated position. We descended to the apartments beneath the building, where, by the aid of torches, we examined little gems of chapels and altars, and beautiful statuary and painting. Down in those dark chambers we were shown a picture of the Judgment, with robbers, murderers, and bad women on the left, and a great array of popes and cardinals on the right. "Why," said one of the company, to the guide, "why not put others on the right as well as popes and cardinals?" "O," said he, with a shrug, "the painter was paid by the Pope to paint it, and he must put them there; he was *paid* for doing it." Although he had a shaven crown, and was an official of the Church, he evidently intimated that some on the right hand might, in truth, have been placed on the left.

Regarded in whatever point of view, save as a house for the true worship of God, St. Peter's is a magnificent building. You are lost in its amplitude, which is sufficient to give room to fifty thousand persons, and you are amazed at its wealth of architecture, statuary, and painting, at which you gaze and wonder, until your sensations of pleasure become oppressive. I visited it often, and always with increasing admiration of its grandeur, proportions, and magnificence; and as I stood taking my last view of it, at the point where I took my first, a feeling of sadness came over me at the reflection that I should never see it again. I had seen other cathedrals before, St. Paul's, Westminster, Nôtre Dame, and have seen others since, including those of Turin, Strasburg, and Cologne, bu[illegible]parison with St. Peter's, they are as the Gram[illegible] the Alps, or as the Falls of the Clyde to Niagara.

And yet, as a house of Christian worship, how utterly offensive to a Protestant! There, conspicuously poised, where all eyes may behold it, in the great nave, and near the high altar, is the bronze statue of St. Peter. It is a sitting figure, resting on a marble pedestal, with an impulsive, stern expression; the right hand raised as if in the act of blessing, and holding two ponderous keys in its left. Save the head and hands, this is the old Jupiter Tonans, with thunder-bolts exchanged for keys. It is a very uncouth affair, and is in striking contrast with the perfection of beauty by which it is surrounded. If the thunder-bolts had only been retained, it would be a good representation of Popery—black, ugly, fierce in aspect, with keys to lock up all heretics, and bolts to strike opponents dead! And to see old women and silly girls, soldiers gilded and plumed, peasants from the Campagna, ladies with liveried servants, and now and then, "few and far between," an ecclesiastic, bowing to this ugly man in bronze, wiping off the kiss of the last worshiper, and then imprinting one of their own on its toe, and rubbing that toe with their foreheads—if all this is not disgusting, I should like to know what is. O, if Peter himself were only there, how he would spurn such silly idolaters from his presence! And while gazing upon the scene, I was informed that, when last in Rome in fiery pursuit of a pair of red stockings, the venerable, pious, retiring, bashful John of New York prostrated himself most profoundly before this image! And yet he was refus[illegible]ed stockings! What ingratitude for such piou[illegible]iation!

And there, too, on all sides, are altars and confession-boxes, where masses are muttered, where sins are confessed and forgiven, for a compensation. At some of these altars I saw masses in progress, without a person to witness them save the boys in waiting; and when the priest was reading from the mass-book, these boys were often playing pranks behind his back! Even in St. Peter's, the mass is falling into the contempt which it merits. Even before the altar, boys are making fun of the priest!

And it was pleasant to see fat-looking priests sitting in their confession-boxes, anxiously waiting for customers, and without finding any! I was struck with the face of one of these fathers, and walked several times in front of his box for the purpose of reading it; but it was too darkly shaded to be legible. I thought he looked at me as if he had caught a fat customer, but he was mistaken. A poor woman came along and dropped on her knees by the side of his box. She looked as if she needed both forgiveness and alms. While whispering into his left ear, another woman came along, and stood at a respectable distance before the box. She dropped courtesies until she attracted the notice of the knight of the box. She then fell on her knees, and soon a long rod like unto a fishing-rod was slowly extended from the box, and thrice laid upon her head. She then crossed herself, rose from her knees, and went smiling away. "And what," said I to our valet, "is the meaning of all this?" "That woman," said he, "is a *little* sinner; perhaps she told a *little* lie, or got a *little* angry, or said some bad word not *big* enough to confess—her so standing before the priest is a confession of some such *little* sin—and he laid the rod upon her in token, and as a sign, of forgiveness." Such was the sight seen, and such was its explanation! What horrible perversion of the Gospel, under the light which comes pouring down the dome of St. Peter's, and in the presence of the high altar, where the Head of the Church alone can officiate! And what a labor-saving process for confession, and to obtain forgiveness! A courtesy is a confession, and the sticking out of a long rod conveys pardon! And all this in St. Peter's! The ridiculous in the presence of the sublime!

With a guide-book in my hand, I was walking around, gazing now at this painting, now at that group of statuary, and now at that superb mosaic. I stopped before the high altar, and by the *confessional*, as it is called, which contains the grave of St. Peter. It is surrounded by a marble balustrade, from which are suspended many lamps constantly burning. A double flight of steps leads down to the shrine, where is a kneeling pope by Canova, and other statues. A silver-gilt box rests upon the tomb of St. Peter, in which are placed the palli, when finished by the withered nuns of St. Agnes, which the Pope confers on the priests when made archbishops. They are placed there to absorb some virtue from the holy atmosphere which there circulates! It is somewhere about this tomb the Pope is said to have hung the badges of office of poor Bishop Ives, on his recent surrender of them, with his faith, at the foot of the sovereign pontiff! Is it not a wonder that sensible men do not see how closely Puseyism treads upon the heels of the ridiculous and farcical!

As I turned away from the "Confessional," I observed a young man of medium appearance, half-way between a peasant and a shop-keeper, making his way to an altar. He knelt before it. I stood to witness the result. He prayed for a brief time. Without changing his position, he looked round and beckoned to a boy. They whispered. The boy ran off, and soon returned with a priest. The wafer was taken out—converted into God—was laid upon the man's tongue—and the priest was away again! The whole thing was over in as short time as it takes me to write this account of it. This was the only instance I saw in Italy of a man taking the wafer. This was in St. Peter's, and the whole thing, as far, at least, as the officials were concerned, was a farce. There is no worship in this basilica of the popes, it is only a splendid temple of the arts.

CHAPTER XXIII.

Sistine.—Fresco of the Judgment.—Entrance of Cardinals.—Entrance of the Pope.—Salutation of the Pope.—His Appearance.—Anecdote of Dr. Miller.—Questions.—Cardinals.—Antonelli.—How to modify our Opinions and Ideas.—How absurd appear the Claims of Popery in the Sistine.

The Sistine Chapel is, of course, an object of great curiosity at Rome. It is connected with the palace of the Vatican, which is adjoining St. Peter's, and is the private chapel of the Pope. You ascend the famous stair-case of Bernini, which is guarded at the foot by "the Swiss Guards," the most fantastical-looking soldiers imaginable, and enter the Sala Regia, a large audience-chamber adorned with fine frescoes, and, among others, with that commemorating the massacre of St. Bartholomew! Papists would deny any responsibility for that horrible massacre, and yet its blessed memory is perpetuated in the Vatican by a splendid fresco! From this chamber you enter the Sistine, and the fresco of the Judgment, by Angelo, sixty feet high and thirty broad, is before you. This is universally admitted to be the most extraordinary picture in the history of the art of painting. The conception is such as the genius alone of Angelo could embody, and the result is grand and sublime. Although faded by the triple effect of damp, time, and the incense so often burned on the altar beneath it, it is difficult to weary in gazing upon it.

This spot we frequently visited; and it was here, at

vespers and matins, on feast-days, we had our views of the Pope and his cardinals. The cardinals enter by the same door as do strangers—walk along the aisle, with a servant untwisting their robes, to the inner of the three apartments into which it is divided—there they kneel and pray toward the altar, their attendants fixing their robes all the while—then they rise, and, after bowing to the altar and to their brethren on the right and left, take their seats, with their servants at their feet.

When all is in preparation, there is a bustle, and soon the Pope enters by the opposite door, bows to the altar, and goes up to his chair. Then one after the other the cardinals leave their seats, their scarlet robes trailing behind them; and after saluting the Pope by kissing his hand covered by his vestments, they return to them. When this ceremony, which fills you with disgust for the actors, is over, the services commence, which are mostly conducted by a choir made up of men and eunuchs. Twice did I witness these ceremonies in the Sistine; on the first occasion there were sixteen, on the second, twenty-three cardinals in attendance. The Pope is a man of fine proportions, six feet two or three inches high, with a pleasing, pensive aspect, not very Italian in a visage which is more expressive of good nature than of talent or firmness. He might do very well to govern a convent; but he is utterly unqualified for his double position as the head of a church and of a state. Personally he is amiable and well-meaning; in morals he stands higher than his predecessors or cardinals; and that is all. While in his presence I thought of an anecdote told of the good

Dr. Miller, of Princeton. When in the Seminary there, I had a fellow-student of far more beauty than brains, and who, like all such, was quite a pretender. An elder from a country church went to the professor to inquire for a pastor, and he named to him several young gentlemen. "I have heard," said the elder, "of Mr. ——," naming the pretty student; "what do you think of him, Dr. Miller?" Not wishing to say any thing against, nor yet willing to commit himself as strongly recommending the student, he hesitated, but finally replied, "*He is a confoundedly good-looking fellow.*" This is about my estimate of Pio Nono. Yet I confess that while gazing upon him, dressed so gorgeously, and receiving so coldly the profound homage of the cardinals, I could not help asking, Is that the man who retired under the pretense of going to pray, dressed himself in the livery of a servant, jumped upon the box of a carriage, and was off to Gaeta? Is that the vicar of Jesus Christ in our world—the head of the visible Church—without a belief in whose claims, and an abject submission to them, I can not enter heaven?

And what shall I say of the cardinals? Some of them were very old, bending under the weight of years; some of them were very plethoric, and quite in danger of apoplexy; and some of them quite young for their position, and good-looking. But none of them so impressed me as did Antonelli, the cardinal Secretary of State. Young, say forty-five—thin, tall, with penetrating eye, and a face strongly expressive of intellect, passion, and will, you would single him from the rest as a real spirit. And such, by all accounts, he is. He is the soul of the College of Cardinals; he is the real Pope, while Pio Nono is a mere puppet in his hands, used simply to give validity and legality to his acts. And he is all his looks indicate; shrewd, far-seeing, vindictive, tyrannical, of an iron will, profuse, and profligate in his morals. Such is his reputation; such is the portrait of him given me by one who knew him well, and for years. There was a crowd in the Sistine on each of the occasions to which I allude; nor was there a person there of any mark that escaped the notice of Antonelli. When the Pope was reading the missal, this cardinal was reading the audience, and I was striving to read the cardinals.

How a few sights like those witnessed in the Sistine modify many of our feelings and opinions! A bishop or archbishop, singly, is quite a person; a single cardinal in a country, as Wiseman in England, is far more so; but when you see them in crowds, as in Rome or Naples, you soon pass them by without notice. When you learn their true character, you despise them; you regard them as does a good man self-righteousness—the more, the worse. With us a living lizard adds to the attraction of a raree-show; but when they surround you every where, as in Italy, they become excessively offensive.

And as you gaze upon the Pope and cardinals in the Sistine, how the idea of infallibility, as taught by the Papists, takes unto itself wings! What, that good-looking, good-natured, but yet not intelligent-looking man, infallible! Believe it who can. What, the Pope, and these cardinals in conclave, infallible! The idea is preposterous. And to *feel* that it is preposterous, nothing is required but to visit the Sistine, and to witness their gorgeous buffoonery, which, if performed without priestly robes, would subject them to the imputation of lunacy. And are these the men who give laws to the papal world—who make bishops and archbishops in America—who send Wiseman, in red stockings, to England—who decide the question as to colleges in Ireland—who turn their people *against* the crown in Britain—*for* the crown in Austria—*against* liberty in Sardinia and Hungary—and *for* it, wherever they can remove let or hinderance to the extension of their ghostly dominion? Yes, these are the very men, parading their man-millinery before you, and claiming to exercise by Divine right an irresponsible power, which, when allowed, lays the world at their feet. And will their claims be allowed? Yes, when the light of truth has ceased its shining—when the Gospel-sun has fallen from its orbit—when the sea has ceased its soundings. If there is a city in the world where Popery can be so read as to be detested, it is Rome; and if there is a spot in Rome where the claims of Popery seem more ridiculous than another, it is where the Pope and cardinals most do congregate. And when I see clever men, in other respects, pleased as a child with a bawble, with the fillets which these priests of the Sistine confer—seeking advice at their hands as to how they are to manage unruly Americans—taking pompous airs upon themselves because of the favors which they confer—placing a dagger before their names, which, if needful, I fear, they would plunge into the very heart of our liberties at their bidding, because of their advancing them up a rung or two in the priestly ladder; and with the broad banner of our country floating over them, acting as the tools and the spies of these Italian ghostly despots, it requires all the generous actings of my nature to maintain for them a particle of respect.

Popery as a system is an enormous falsehood; may God save America from its deceivings and its tools. To wipe out every suspicion from the mind that there may be some truth in the high claims of the Pope and his college of cardinals, nothing is necessary but a visit to the Sistine. The person who can not be thus cured, is a fit subject for the solemn procession of donkeys which seek the blessing of his holiness on the Feast of St. Antony.

CHAPTER XXIV.

Prodigies of Roman History.—Rome yet a City of Prodigies.—Juggle of St. Januarius. — Holy House of Loretto. — Bambino. — Scala Sancta.—Maria Maggiore.—Statue of Mary at St. Agostine.—Holy Chain in St. Peter's, in Vinculo.—Well in St. Maria, in Via Lata.—Prayer in the Church of St. Gregory.—Popery a prodigious Falsehood.

ROME has been always a city of prodigies; prodigies abound in Roman history from its earliest annals. Æneas was the son of Venus, a goddess. Led by the god Mercurius, he fled from Troy. This god built for him a ship, in which he put to sea with his company. The ship was miraculously conducted to Latium; on landing, he was conducted by a white sow to the place of his first habitation. When the race of Anchises seemed destined to extinction, the god Mars interposed, and by Sylvia, then a vestal, became the father of Romulus and Remus. Sylvia and her two boys were cast into the Tiber; Sylvia became a goddess, and the wife of the god of the river. Her two boys were stranded near the Palatine Hill, and were taken by a she-wolf to her cave, who fed them as a mother. When they needed something more than milk, meat was brought them by a woodpecker, and other birds of augury hovered round the mouth of the cave to keep off insects from the sons of Mars! When Rome was to be built, these two brothers were divided in opinion as to the location; but the flight of vultures decided for the Palatine Hill and for Romulus. Remus was killed by his brother for contemptuously stepping over a rampart made by him around the hill; but subsequently announced his forgiveness of his brother, on the condition of the institution of a feast to commemorate his memory, and on which *a kind of a mass* should be said for the repose of his soul. In a battle with the Sabines the Romans were flying before them; but Romulus called upon Jupiter, and vowed to build him a temple if he would give him victory. The Romans returned to the conflict, gained the victory, and hence the temple of Jupiter Stator. Romulus was taken to heaven by his father Mars in a thunder-storm; where he was worshiped as a god, under the name of Quirinus. But the time would fail me to tell of the prodigies of the pious Numa—of the shower of stones on Mount Alba—of the eagle taking away the cap of Lucumo, and replacing it—of Altus cutting a whetstone with a razor—of the flames that played round the head of the infant Servius—of the statue of Servius rebuking his impious daughter—of the fresh bleeding head dug up on the Capitoline Hill in preparing the foundations for the fanes of Jupiter, Juno, and Minerva—and of the thousand and one wonders which abound in the history of regal, consular, and imperial Rome.

Nor is the city of the seven hills less a city of prodigies now than in the days of augury, pagan priests, speaking statues, and heads bleeding afresh when dug from under the mountains. However the chain of succession, in other respects, has been broken—in this respect it has been prodigiously maintained. Prodigies, prodigies, meet you every where in Italy, and priests and bishops are every where found to swear to their truth; and when the Pope says Amen, then these prodigies become matters of Catholic faith. Of the juggle about the liquefaction of the blood of St. Januarius at Naples, I have already said something. O what a shameful hoax! and now practiced thrice or four times a year, to confirm the vulgar belief!

And there is the "Holy House of Loretto," a peevish and nervous compound of stone and wood, which flew from Palestine to Dalmatia, and then from Dalmatia across the Adriatic to Lauretum, in Italy, in which there is a miraculous image of Mary, which has performed more miracles than Moses, Christ, and all the apostles together. And there is the picture of Mary, faded, dark, and ugly at the present day, at whose fane thousands and tens of thousands now yearly offer up their adorations! And all the lying legends about this rickety house are endorsed by the Right Reverend P. R. Kenrick, of St. Louis, a foreign priest who has come commissioned from Rome to enlighten the ignorant and unconverted Americans! What an enlightened people we will be when our credulity has grown so as to exercise a full faith in such a monster absurdity.

And there is the wonderful Bambino, which mine own eyes have seen, in the church of Ara Cœli, on the Capitoline Hill, and in reference to which I have already said something to Chief-justice Taney. It is a doll, which looks as if it was made in Germany and dressed in Italy, representing the infant Christ. Its history is, of course, miraculous. It was made in Palestine—was lost at sea—suddenly appeared at Leghorn—was conducted in triumph to Rome—was stolen away by a pious lady—was restored by angels to its place again in Ara Cœli, amid the ringing of bells, and at this hour gets more fees, and *is said* to cure more patients, than all the doctors of Rome! The richly-jeweled doll is conveyed in a sumptuous carriage, attended by priests and guards, to the houses of the sick; if they get well, Bambino has the credit; if they die, it has none of the blame! Where, in the pagan and fabulous annals of Rome, is a prodigy to surpass Bambino?

And there is the Scala Sancta, at St. John Lateran. This, too, has its miraculous history. It consists of twenty-eight marble steps, which, tradition says, belonged to the house of Pilate, and down which the Savior descended when he left the judgment-seat. It was carried by angels to Rome, as the house of Loretto was carried to Dalmatia, and thence to Italy. None are permitted to go up these steps save on their knees; and by doing so, the person secures certain plenary indulgences, and for years together. I saw with sorrow devotees crawling up these steps. My feet trod upon the three upper steps, and behold, I yet live! It was crawling up these very steps that the great doctrine of justification by faith burst upon the mind of Luther, with a brightness which was never eclipsed. It is one of the great prodigies of Rome.

And there is the fine basilica of St. Maria Maggiore, so called from being the chief church of Rome dedicated to Mary. It is upon the Esquiline Hill, and upon the very ground selected for the purpose by heaven, and indicated by a fall of snow covering precisely the ground, on the 5th day of August! Can the shower of stones on Mount Alba surpass this? Beneath an altar in this church are the swaddling-clothes which covered the Savior when laid in the manger! Are not these prodigies?

In the church of St. Agostine is a statue of Mary and the infant Savior, by Sansovino. It possesses great sanctity and efficacy; but why, I could not learn. I saw crowds of poor people kissing the toe of Mary, and rendering the most revolting homage to the statuary! And the church, its naves, its pillars, its altars, are glittering all over with hearts hung on them by the persons who obtained healing by kissing the toe of Mary, and rendering homage to the marble representation of herself and her Son!

In the church of St. Peter's, in Vinculo, is the chain which bound St. Peter when in prison in Jerusalem. That holy chain gives its name to the building, and imparts to it its sanctity. Its very touch has wrought many miracles. Filings from it have been sold at enormous prices, and have been set in rings, bracelets, and pins for kings and queens. Five devils flew out of the mouth of a man on being touched with it; and, being broken in two, it became miraculously one again on being put into the hands of the Pope by St. Helena! And these miracles are splendidly commemorated by frescoes from the pencils of the best masters. And that wondrous chain is annually exhibited for the adoration of the faithful. Is not that chain a prodigy? And beneath the church of St. Maria, in Via Lata, is the miraculous well, which sprung up for the baptism of those converted by Paul, and the very pillar to which he was bound, and the very chain that bound him to it! And that miraculous water is kept under lock and key, and is only exhibited to the faithful once a year! On that pillar these words are deeply engraven, "*Verbum Dei non est alligatum.*" O, if that sentence was only engraved on the pillar which adorns the piazza of St. Peter's!

But what impressed me beyond any thing of the kind I saw in Rome, was a prayer offered by the faithful daily in the church of St. Gregory. There is among the priests great expectations as to the return of England to the true faith, which the numerous defections there have greatly increased. And St. Gregory is the personage to whom they most look, and whose aid they most solicit to this end. And here is the prayer, copied on the spot from a little board on which it is pasted, in Italian and English, for the use of the faithful:

"O adorable defender and propagator of the faith, St. Gregory, from thy seat of glory in heaven, behold how great a portion of the noblest British empire is without the pale of that holy faith, which through thy zeal it received of the sons of Saint Benedict, sent thither by thee; and how other regions of this miserable world are in danger of losing this most precious of divine gifts. Through that most ardent charity which during life animated thee, obtain for that kingdom, from the Most High, the increase and diffusion of the Catholic faith; and for us the grace that we may never waver in the true faith, which would be the most severe chastisement that could befall us for the punishment of our sins. Amen."

Was ever a prayer offered to Jupiter by Romulus more purely pagan than this?

And were it necessary to adduce the old relics of St. Peter's, St. John Lateran, Santa Croce, the miraculous bones, clothes, stones, and pictures that every where abound, it would appear that Rome is at this hour more a city of prodigies than when Numa presided in the state, or when the Pontifex Maximus offered sacrifices, or augurs predicted coming events from the entrails of animals or the flight of birds. Popery is a religion of prodigies, and is itself a prodigy of falsehood. To me it is a wonder how any sensible man can do otherwise than scornfully reject it.

CHAPTER XXV.

Rome to be studied.—Its numerous Churches.—Their Riches of Art and Endowment.—Numerous Priests and Nuns.—Poverty of the People.—Abounding Beggars.—Way to shake them off.—Absence of Youth.—The People in Fear.—Despotism, through the Confessional.—Its Morals.—No Religion there.—The Voice of Rome to the Nations.—Its History not yet ended.

To an American and a Christian visiting Rome, all questions pertaining to its moral and social condition possess deep interest; and they will receive a full examination. Rome is the centre of Papal unity — is the seat of the Pope and his court—is the Jerusalem of the Papist in all lands—is the point whence all the authority in the Papal Church proceeds, and whither all questions, of whatever character upon which the provinces are divided, return for solution. There is the fountain-head of infallibility, and where you would very naturally expect those model civil and social institutions to exist after which the Pope and his priests would fashion the world. And if the nations could only read in the light of history, and in the light of the present state of Rome and the Romans, the true, the legitimate influence of Popery wherever it gains the ascendant power, they would dread its establishment among them as they would the scourges of war, famine, and pestilence.

Among the first things that impress you in Rome is the number and splendor of its churches. The people are about one hundred and fifty thousand all told, and there are said to be nearly four hundred churches. This would be a church for every four hundred inhabitants. And when we consider that St. Peter's, St. John Lateran, St. Maria Maggiore, would contain many thousands, and that even the smaller churches would contain from one to three thousand, we will readily admit that there is a superabundance of church accommodation.

And these churches are all richly, many of them magnificently embellished. There is a wealth of art in its churches, almost if not quite sufficient to pay the debt of the English nation. And these churches, with their cardinals, archbishops, bishops, chapters, and priests, are utterly independent of the people; they are all richly, some of them royally endowed.

Another of the striking peculiarities of Rome is the number of its priests and nuns. There are upward of two thousand nuns, and about three thousand priests; making a due allowance for children, there is a priest for every twenty-five adults! And, taken as a class, they are the best-looking, best-dressed, best-fed men you meet; and if they are not perfectly satisfied with their condition, their stately tread, their self-complacent air, bear false witness against them. The Pope lives in regal style. The cardinals, with their horses, servants, carriages all in scarlet, live and move as princes. They are the princes of the Church and of the Roman state. The bishops live sumptuously; and even the mendicant monks are as fat and greasy as is desirable. And such is the number of these priests that you meet them every where; and when a noted service is to be performed, they are there in dozens as actors. If priests of every class and character, in numbers entirely satisfactory, and wielding all power, could civilize, enlighten, and Christianize a place, then, in every desirable respect, Rome would be an earthly paradise.

But in striking contrast with the sumptuousness of their churches, their riches of art, and the wealth of the priests, is the poverty and wretchedness of the people. Beggars meet you every where—in the streets, at the doors of cafés and shops, at the doors of churches, amid the ruins of the Forum and the Coliseum, and even under the very dome of St. Peter's. While leaning over the "confessional" and admiring the kneeling Pope, by Canova, a mutilated beggar gave me a gentle hint, by politely pulling the tail of my coat, that charity should be exercised under the shadow of the high altar, and in the very presence of the holy relics of Peter and Paul! All points of interest which attract strangers have also peculiar attraction for beggars. They annoy you every where, and are shaken off with difficulty. An English gentleman, the companion of many a ramble, I found, by a stamp of his foot and the utterance of certain sounds, could send them off at once. After witnessing his tact frequently, and after calling him a few times to my aid, I asked him what he said. "I do not know," he said, laughingly; "I but strive to imitate the action and words of a priest before whom I saw the beggars flee, the other day, in the Corso." We appealed to our valet for the interpretation, who said they meant "Go to the d—." No wonder the poor creatures so hastily concluded that the person who could send them so far beyond Purgatory would give them neither a paul nor a penny.

You also miss from the streets and promenades of Rome the joyous youth, ranging from fourteen to twenty-five, which you meet every where in Britain and France; and the people you do meet seem dull and joyless. They seem to walk in dread of an omnipresent enemy. And instead of bowing to the priests that are evermore flitting along with shovel-hats and robes indicating their order, they dart on them a furtive glance, and give a meaning shake of the head when they are past. You need only walk the streets, enter the shops, and read the countenances of the people, to know that the Romans feel and dread the rod of the oppressor.

Nor is there any liberty in Rome. Every family is under a priestly spy: through the confessional and the women the priest gets the secrets of the family, its visitors, the opinions of fathers and sons; and often, on the confessions of mothers and daughters, husbands and brothers are immured in prisons, or sentenced to the galleys. A gentleman, for years a resident of the city, informed me that the despotism of the worst emperors was no more severe than that now exercised under the sanction of Pio Nono. Rome, Naples, Austria, par excellence Papal states, and yet the culminating points of despotism!

Nor are there any true morals in Rome. How could there be with such an army of lazy priests, and with such a swarm of French soldiers? The last Pope has left several heirs: the present one has a good public character; but as to the cardinals and priests, it is notorious that they are only forbidden to marry. The noblest of the Romans say that, because of the utter profligacy of the priests and their arts at the confessional, they have no confidence in the virtue of their wives, mothers, sisters, or daughters! If such is the public and general character of the priests, what must be that of the people? Indeed, I could not place before my readers the statements made, and by the very best witnesses, for the purpose of illustrating the low point to which morals have fallen in Rome, and through the profligacy of the clergy, from the Pope down to the miserable mendicant friar, whose character is often more filthy than his feet or his frock.

Nor is there any religion in Rome. There is superstition there as rife as in the days when Jupiter and Venus were worshiped; but, as a rule, the religion of Christ is unknown and unpracticed. I spent a Sabbath there; and as there was no Protestant worship save that of the Puseyitish stamp without the walls, and as I prefer the reality to the bungling imitation, I went to St. Peter's, and other churches. The markets and shops were more crowded than usual. The priests were seen every where trading. Peasants from beyond the walls, in every variety of costume, were in the streets. The Sistine was crowded mostly by strangers to see the Pope at mass amid the glittering swords of the "guard noble;" but St. Peter's was almost deserted, as were the other churches that I visited. There is no Sabbath in Rome—there is no Bible influence in Rome; the common people scarcely know it by name—there is no preaching of the Gospel in Rome—there is no instruction of the young into the principles of Divine truth. Their religious literature is a compilation of lying legends, of which the wonders of Bambino and of the Holy House of Loretto are good samples; and priests and people are living without hope and without God in the world. I have not a doubt but that the priests are mainly infidels; and that the people, who are not like the priests, are mainly idolaters, from whose minds all ideas of God and of Christ are crowded out by fictions concerning Peter, pictures, holy relics and places, fables of the saints, and, more than all and above all, by Mary and Bambino.

Some may say this picture is overdrawn; but it is not even one half to the reality. So all will say who have spent a month in Rome truly desirous to know its social and moral state. Your liberty, your property, your life, hang suspended upon the will of priests, who are at once ignorant, superstitious, rapacious, and profligate, who feel that they have a divine warrant to flay or fleece you as they will, and who yield to no impulse save that which tends to strengthen their claims and to extend their dominion. And these Romish priests form the great central power of the Papal Church. They make, or unmake, bishops and archbishops; and they send out decrees binding upon all their people, and as unchangeable as the laws of the Medes, which give direction and form to the movements and opinions of all their priests to the ends of the earth. And could these priests have their way, they would lay the nations, chained and debased, as lowly at the feet of the Pope and his cardinals as the once imperial city of the Cæsars now lies. From its crowded prisons, and its betrayed people, and its banished patriots, and its Christless churches—from its noiseless streets, and the ruins which crowd its ancient hills, and its men afraid to lisp their opinions to their wives or daughters, a voice rises for the warning of the nations, saying, "THE PRICE OF YOUR CIVIL AND RELIGIOUS LIBERTY IS ETERNAL VIGILANCE OF POPERY."

The history of Rome is not ended. It is yet the seat of empire in opposition to the kingdom of God. It is the centre of a spiritual power felt for evil to the ends of the earth. Let that power be scattered, and its prestige is gone—let it be rendered subservient to truth, and the world would feel its renovating effects. God has his eye upon Rome, and, priest-ridden and down-trodden as it is, will make it subservient to some glorious end. For Popery there is nothing in reserve but destruction; like a leprous Jewish house, it must be torn down. But moral conquests may yet be obtained on the banks of the muddy Tiber which will throw those of all the Cæsars into the shade.

CHAPTER XXVI.

Leaving Rome.—A Procession of the Host.—The Aurelian Way.—Civita Vecchia.—Genoa from the Sea.—The City.—Columbus.—Political History.—Duomo.—Head of John the Baptist.—Sacro Catino.—Santa Maria.—An Evening Ramble.—Scenes in the Streets—Female Dress.—Tastes differ.

THE time had come for our departure from Rome. As we wound our way through the narrow and dirty streets toward the bridge St. Angelo, we met a procession carrying the host to a dying man. Our carriage stopped, and our postillions uncovered, as did all the people in the street. A guard of soldiers went before it with drawn swords; a priest gorgeously arrayed carried it, followed by one of those hideous processions made up of persons wrapped up in a sheet with holes made only for their eyes; another guard of soldiers brought up the rear! Nothing but its stupendous wickedness can surpass its stupendous folly and gross superstition. We crossed the noble bridge, filed to the left in front of the castle of St. Angelo, passed by the Via S. Spirito, under the walls of St. Peter's, and by the Fabrician Gate made our exit from the City of the Popes. And as the magnificent dome of St. Angelo died away in the distance, and the gathering shades of evening hid one object after another from our view, we yielded to a feeling of melancholy, suggested by the reflection that we had taken our last view of the ruins, the splendor, the wretchedness, and the superstition of the most historic, the most superstitious, the most dilapidated, the worst governed city on the globe. It is pleasant to visit Rome; it would be horrible to live there.

We left Rome about seven o'clock in the evening, and after trundling all night over the old Aurelian Way, and through as desolate a country as could be desired, so far as we could see it by the light of a full moon, we found ourselves entering the ponderous gates of Civita Vecchia at five in the morning. This is the sea-port of Rome, and is in every respect as contemptible as it has been represented. Soldiers, priests, beggars, here swarm as they do every where in Italy. Why is it that these always abound together? We took a walk around the city—through the market, its churches, and around its fortifications. Nothing impressed us. It was on the balcony of a hotel here, overlooking the square, that an Italian denounced to me the priests and soldiers sauntering below, in thoughts that breathed and words that burned. The steamer from Naples soon made her appearance, and we were soon away for Genoa.

Genoa looks magnificently from the sea. It lies at the base of a broken range of hills gracefully sloping to the water, and whose sides are dotted with gay suburban palaces almost to the very summit. Its streets are very narrow, exceedingly up and down, in many places inaccessible to carriages, and several of them are lined with palaces. Indeed, it is called "the City of Palaces." But while we by no means admired it to the extent we expected and intended, it is a city of deep interest to a traveler from America. It was here that Columbus was born, the discoverer of the Western World. The son of a poor wool-comber, he soon developed an irresistible passion for the sea. At the age of fourteen he commenced navigating these waters, and when he had passed but a little beyond his fiftieth year, he gave rise to a new era in the history of our race by the discovery of America. And yet little is known here of the man, who, in the estimation of the civilized world, is one of the great and chief benefactors of mankind. He bequeathed a few manuscripts to the city—these are venerated as relics, and that is all! I asked for the place where the wool-comber lived, but none could tell me.

The political history of Genoa makes it also interesting to an American. After the downfall of the empire of Charlemagne, it became a republic, and famous for its maritime enterprise. The conflicts between it and Venice are known of all men. But although often torn by fearful internal dissensions, and often conquered by foreign powers, and now a part and parcel of the kingdom of Sardinia, its old love of liberty has never been extinguished. It is now the house of refuge for the banished patriots of Lower Italy; and while the cities of the Pope and of the King of Naples are rapidly declining, this is rapidly rising, and looks more like an American city as to the shipping in the harbor, the bustle on the quays, and the warehouses erecting, than any other we have seen on the Mediterranean.

Genoa is a Papal city, while the law secures the rights of conscience to all. The priests and churches are very numerous, but the priests walk not as proudly, nor are the churches as gorgeous, as in Central Italy.

The Duomo or Cathedral of St. Lorenzo is a singular affair, different in its architecture from any we saw. In its friezes are inscriptions which narrate that the city was founded by a grandson of Noah, and that James II., prince of Troy, took possession of it! Priests have a remarkably fine genius for making history. Here also is a neat chapel, which no woman is permitted to enter, beneath whose altar is a chest containing the head of St. John the Baptist! Women were excluded by Pope Innocent VIII. from this sacred chapel in vengeance upon Herodias. Why were not men also excluded in vengeance upon the executioner? We were only permitted to see the chest—we dare not look with Protestant eyes upon the holy head! How many heads the preacher in the wilderness must have had! Here also is a miraculous painting, by Luke, of Mary and Bambino. If Luke painted all the pictures ascribed to him, we see not how he got time to write his Gospel or to say his prayers. One thing is certain, he was a very miserable artist. But, above all, here is the wonderful Sacro Catino, a precious dish said to have been given by the Queen of Sheba to Solomon, to have held the Paschal Lamb at the Last Supper, and to be the very cup in which Joseph of Arimathea caught the blood flowing from the wounds of the Savior on the cross! Three times a year is this Catino brought out, amid an array of priestly magnificence, for the veneration and adoration of the faithful. It is a glass cup brought from Palestine by the Crusaders, and pious priests have made its history. It was once taken to Paris, where it was broken; but the pieces were put together with gold, which made it the more valuable. The priests offered to show us the sacred relic for five francs a head, but not considering the gross humbug worth the price, we declined the bargain.

From St. Lorenzo, we clambered up a high hill, on which is situated the church of Santa Maria di Carignano, and wound our way up to the very summit of its superb cupola. The city, the harbor, the sea, lay beneath us, and the magnificent environs lay around and above us. The view is neither grand nor extended, but Italy presents none more beautiful.

In the cool of the day, we sallied out to see and hear what we could. We entered every church we met, and it was the same old story—beggars at the door—a few women inside—priests—altars—pictures, some good, some not—the same monotonous mumbling of the mass, and here and there an old man praying before crosses and pictures. Recognized as strangers, we were assailed by beggars at every corner, among whom was a fair sprinkling of shaven crowns, with dirty monkish garbs. And to see priests, peasants, and women stopping in the midst of their prayers, talking and laughing, and then starting on again without ever changing their kneeling position—the whole thing reveals a heartlessness which can not be described to those who have never witnessed it. The Rev. Mr. L., of Massachusetts, just returning from a visit to the East, was one of the company. He stated that the Greek Church in the East was even worse than the Church in Italy; and that if in Jerusalem he must be one or the other, he would prefer being a Mohammedan to a Christian after the Greek or Roman stamp; that the Turk held and practiced more of the truths of the Bible, than did the one or the other! How can the Turks be converted to Popery?

The streets were crowded with people, and mountebanks were playing in every direction, and some of them performing wonderful feats. We were impressed strongly with the beauty and the dress of the females. Light in frame, with dark hair and eyes, and finely proportioned, they seemed, in the gloaming of the day, rather to float than to walk before you. They wear no bonnets—a bonnet is a sure sign of a foreigner. Their dress consists of a piece of muslin folded across the top of the head, and elegantly pinned to the hair, and gracefully falling around the neck and over the shoulders in the form of a shawl. Their ear-rings are usually large and elegant. Their countenances are brilliant and expressive, and although singular in dress and appearance, you remember only their taste and elegance. We saw no female dress in Europe that we desired to see introduced into our country, save that of the ladies of Genoa. On the evening of a warm summer's day, it would be cool, modest, and exceedingly graceful. They would be an excellent substitute for those excuses for bonnets which hang upon the rear of a lady's head, or for that enormously ugly superfluity of Leghorn under which they sometimes walk, which keeps all companions at a respectful distance, and which flaps in the wind like an umbrella from which the whalebone had been taken away. Hideous affairs! Tastes, how various! Fashion, what a tyrant!

CHAPTER XXVII.

Departure from Genoa.—A Procession.—The Goddess of the City.—Primitive Work.—Ascent of the Apennines.—Descent.—Degraded Woman.—Novi.—Great Valley, and fertile.—Alessandria.—Marengo: its Battle.—Dessaix.—Austria.—Haynau an Incarnation of Austria.—Enter Turin.—An Incident.

In leaving the city for Turin, we had an enchanting view of Genoa and its harbor. On our way out we passed one of those horrible funeral processions, such as we had met in Naples and Rome, in which persons are covered with sheets, with holes only for their eyes! As we passed through the gate of the strong wall that guards the city, we turned back to read the inscription over it, from which we learned that "The most blessed Virgin" is its guardian goddess! Soon we came to a point where we took our last view of the Mediterranean, and turned into a valley of beautiful cultivation, and pursued our way to the foot of the Apennines. The day was hot and the road dusty, and it was quite primitive and refreshing to see men scattering water on the highways with shovels from the little streamlets that flowed on either side of them! No ideas of labor-saving machinery have yet reached Italy, save those which pertain to the doing up of confessions, and forgiving sins, and getting money. In inventions for these purposes, it leads the world.

We ascended the Apennines by a winding road of stupendous workmanship, which is at no point steep, although it winds up a mountain which seems to possess no more inclination from a straight line than does the leaning tower of Pisa. As we looked up we could see nothing but wall above wall, and arch above arch, as high as the eye could reach; and yet, drawn by twelve horses driven and ridden by quite a guard of postillions, we ascended in full trot to the summit; and as we looked down, we could see carriages and men as pigmies in the profound depths below! On the very summit of the mountain, where nothing but monks and goats can live, we found a monastery whose bell was tolling as we passed it. The sound recalled far distant lands, and a well-remembered house of prayer, and a beloved people accustomed to repair to the sanctuary at the call of the church-going bell! We thought, silently prayed, and passed on. And if we went up the Apennines in a full trot, how can I describe the manner we went down it? A full gallop does not express it as we felt it. And amid clouds of dust, the jabbering of postillions, the baying of dogs at our John Gilpin career, we traveled down, and on to Novi.

They were tunneling the Apennines for a railway from Turin to Genoa, which, when completed, will be a great affair for Sardinia. And armies of women were engaged in making these tunnels! With a pannier of peculiar construction, made to fit the back, they entered the tunnel at one side, and emerged, laded, on the other side; bent down like beasts of burden, they followed each other in rows to the end of the embankment, where each turned round; there a man drew a pin which let the bottom fall out, and the stone, gravel, or clay fell out of the basket! And hundreds of women were working in this way at this bestial employment! Lime-kilns, in great number, line the road; and the women were quarrying the stones, carrying them to the kilns, and sending away the lime! Whether these women were convicts, or the wives and daughters of the peasants, I know not; but they wore no criminal badge. This was the lowest state of female degradation I ever beheld. Can the world furnish a lower? And in these parts of Sardinia there are no "godless schools" to vex the priests or to pervert the people.

Out of the large cities, the inns of Italy are wretched. We dined at Novi, and spent some hours there waiting the cars. The people looked extremely poor, and the town extremely dirty. All the memorial I find in my journal in reference to this place is, "At Novi we dined at the table d'hôte, and most filthy it was." Here we took the railway, and found it a most pleasant change from the diligence in which we came rushing down the Apennines like an avalanche. We flew over a plain of boundless extent, level as our salt meadows or Western prairies, reaching from the Apennines to the Alps, crowded with villages under magnificent cultivation, and irrigated from both ranges. We were informed that by means of irrigation three crops are annually raised on this plain. In the midst of it stands the city of Alessandria, which has a history. This city is near the junction of the Tanaro and Bormido, and the country around is often overflown by these rivers, and may be overflown by them at any time when necessary. It was this fact which led to its selection for a fortress in the days of the Guelfs and the Ghibellines. It was called Alessandria after Pope Alexander of blessed memory, who, it is said, placed his foot upon the neck of the Emperor Frederic, appropriating and quoting the text, "Thou shalt tread upon the lion and the adder." The Emperor answered, "Not to you, but to Peter;" the Pope replied, "To me, and to Peter." But the great interest of this place to the modern traveler is, that the famous battle of Marengo was fought in its vicinity, one of the great battles of Napoleon. On that extended plain, on the 13th of June, 1800, met the Austrians under Melas, forty thousand strong, and the French under Napoleon, numbering only twenty thousand. The battle was protracted and desperate. The French ranks broke, and were retreating, when Dessaix appeared in the distance. Riding up to Bonaparte, he said, "I think this a battle lost." "I think it a battle won," was the reply. Thinking they were masters of the field, the Austrians relaxed their exertions, and gave way to the most clamorous joy; when Napoleon, returning upon them unexpectedly, drove all before him. Hundreds were slain—thousands were taken prisoners. The Bormido was bridged with the dead bodies of horses and men, and rolled red with their blood. And there, under our eyes, lay the extended plain, bearing the most luxuriant crops, where this fearful conflict took place; and all, save the massive fortifications of the city, looked as calmly and as quietly as if "the battle of the warrior with confused noise, and garments rolled in blood," had never been there fought. The way in which the Little Corporal gained this battle would almost induce the belief that the stars in their courses fought with him. Never was he so near losing a battle that he did not lose, and rarely did he gain so complete a victory. But it was gained at the expense of the life of the gallant and generous Dessaix, to whom even the Egyptians gave the name of the *Just Sultan*, who fell by a cannon-ball just as the shouts of victory rose from the ranks of the French. His body was embalmed and carried to the hospitium on the St. Bernard, where stands a monument erected to his memory. Another was erected to him on the plain of Marengo, which was destroyed by the Austrians in 1814. Will Austria ever do a noble act? It is essentially a nation of savages, and should be so regarded and treated. Its history is a disgrace to the civilization of Europe. I can not otherwise regard the human butcher Haynau than as Austria incarnate. It would seem as if the highest welfare of our race, and especially the true social regeneration of Europe, require that it should be broken to pieces as a potter's vessel.

From Alessandria we proceeded onward toward Turin. Soon the Alps, which lay all day in dim outline propping the sky, became clearly visible. As the intense glare of the sun faded away on the approach of evening, they became clearly defined. As we approached them the oppressive heat of the day gave way to a chilly atmosphere, which rendered an overcoat quite comfortable. As the dusk of the evening fell around us, we crossed the Po, and under the dazzling glare of snow-clad mountains, on which a bright, full, cloudless moon was shining, we entered the city of Turin, and soon found ourselves comfortably located in the Hotel l'Europe. We were now in the beautiful capital of the kingdom of Sardinia.

At a station between Alessandria and Turin, two brawny yet well dressed Italians came, jostling each other, into our car. Soon they commenced an excited conversation, which became an intense scold. There would be an occasional lull, but they would commence again with increased fury. We expected a fight; but it was all words, and the less interesting because we could not understand them. My traveling friend had a severe headache, which was not made better by the noise of our neighbors; and when suffering was no longer a virtue, he jumped convulsively to his feet, and poured such a torrent of indignation in English upon them as perfectly astounded them. Napoleon at Marengo made no more bold or sudden attack! They looked at my friend, and, after exchanging an indignant glance at one another, the war ceased. Not another word did they utter. Soon one of them left us; the other accompanied us to Turin, and was quite attentive to us when we reached the station there. And when in our subsequent wanderings we met with any thing unpleasant, I frequently advised my friend to try the virtue of a bluster in English. Judging by the effect on this occasion, our language must possess great energy to those who do not understand it.

CHAPTER XXVIII.

Turin.—Beautiful for Situation.—No Antiquities.—Growing rapidly. —Charles Albert deceived.—His Death.—Room in the Palace.—Spirit of the present King.—Opposed by the Priests.—Legislature of Turin.—Senate and House.—Our Chargé at Turin.—Santo Sudario.—Worship with the Waldenses: their Chapel.—A Royal People: their Doctrines and Order.—Turin a strong Point from which to act on Italy.

TURIN is a beautiful city, the most grandly situated of any inland capital in Europe. It has no suburbs, and you enter at once from a perfect country into the streets of a beautiful city. The transition seems like magic. Through the perspective of the streets, which are wide, and cross each other at right angles, the hills, the mountains, *the Alps*, which surround the city, are constantly in view. There, on the one side, is Monte Cenis and Monte Viso, clothed in perpetual snow, calmly looking down upon you, and cooling even the noonday heat by their cold breath; and on the other flows the classic Po, a deep and rapid river. Beyond the Po, and immediately fronting the city, rises the Collina, a beautiful range of hills sloping to the river, and sparkling with beautiful villas to its very summit. At a short distance from the city, and as part of the Collina, rises Moncalieri, which is surmounted by a royal palace, the favorite country residence of the present royal family. Indeed, every beauty which can be afforded by wood, water, mountain, and plain; by city and country; by a most luxuriant vegetation in the presence of eternal snows, are combined in the neighborhood of Turin! We doubt whether it is equaled by any inland city of the world for beauty of situation.

Turin, unlike Naples, Rome, and Genoa, has but few historic associations. It has almost no antiques, classical or mediæval, so frequently has it been ravaged by the surrounding powers, which have so frequently contended for it. Now the capital of the kingdom of Sardinia, almost the only constitutional government in continental Europe, it is growing almost with the rapidity of an American city. The persecuted Christians and patriots of Central and Southern Italy flock there for protection; and as they bring with them property, intelligence, industry, and a love of liberty, the city is rapidly rising. New streets are making, and blocks of houses are there rising, as in the city of New York. The appearance of every thing around you makes you feel that you have passed beyond the blasting, crushing influence of the priest, and that you are among a people strongly imbued with the principles of liberty and Protestantism. And so you are.

The recent King of Sardinia, Charles Albert, headed, in 1848 and 1849, what was called the Italian League, whose object was to combine the various states of Italy into an Italian empire. Lombardy, Naples (and perhaps the States of the Church), entered cordially into the League; but bloody Austria opposed, and declared war against it. Lombardy and Naples treacherously withheld the forces promised, and Charles Albert was defeated. He resigned his throne to his son on the field of battle, and retired to Spain, where he died of a broken heart. And there, in a room in the palace, is the bed on which he died, and the furniture of the room in which his broken heart ceased its pulsations; and but few moderate American farmers would consider the bed or furniture too sumptuous for their own sleeping apartments. The son, into whose hands he surrendered the government, now reigns in Turin, with more than the feelings of his father glowing in his soul. He is dead against Austria—is the friend of civil and religious liberty—maintains the Constitution granted by his father with vigor—is hated by the old despotisms around him, whose ministers at his court are spies on his conduct; and is yet destined to act a conspicuous part in the affairs of Italy. So resolute is he in maintaining his position, that he openly declares that the power which prostrates the constitutional liberty of his people must first march over his lifeless corpse. Of course, this is wormwood and gall to the priests, whose instincts are all for despotism and darkness. They have opposed in every way the progress of free institutions in Piedmont, and, as a reward for their opposition, some of their bishops are in banishment, and they are all hated at home. The world is rapidly learning that the great object and aim of Popery is to maintain the power and dominion of the priest. The Romish priesthood is a corporation of cenobites, closely compacted and bound together by the strong ties of self-interest, whose object is to retain and maintain, and transmit their corporate power by all and by any means.

The Senate and House of Deputies, modeled after

the British House of Lords and Commons, were in session in Turin. This is the only legislative body in Italy! The Senate is appointed by the king and his ministers; the Delegates are elected by the people. And their laws are laws. With cautious but steady progress, they are reforming old abuses, laying aside old feudal institutions, and laying a deep and broad foundation for a political and social fabric like unto that of England. There is a strong democratic element in the House of Deputies, whose leaders are its best orators. Never did we see a more nobly-developed company of men assembled, or, to appearance, more intelligent or gentlemanly, than the Senate of Sardinia; and the House of Deputies was as sedate and orderly, as was that of France, as I have already described it, disorderly and turbulent. We were rejoiced to find that at such a formative and critical period in it's history our government was there represented by the Honorable William B. Kinney, a gentleman every way competent to discharge the high duties of his mission. We have reason to know that he is in high favor with the court, and with the noble men who are seeking to fortify the free institutions of their country. His mission to Turin will not be in vain.

We spent a Sabbath in this city which will not soon be forgotten. Drums were beating, and soldiers marching in all directions in the morning. About ten o'clock we went to the Cathedral, not to hear or see mass, of which we had seen and heard enough for a thousand years, nor yet so much to see the royal family, which was there, as to visit the chapel of the Santo Sudario, the priestly glory of Turin. But what is the

Santo Sudario? It is nothing less than one of the three folds of the shroud in which Joseph of Arimathea wrapped the body of Jesus! and which to this hour bears the impress of his body! The other two folds are at Rome and Besançon. This wonderfully sacred relic was discovered during the Crusades—was first deposited in Chambéry; but was sent to Turin to enable St. Borromeo to venerate it without the trouble of crossing the Alps! It seems they never returned it. And there is its magnificent chapel in the Duomo, where the old rag is exhibited for the veneration of the people on great occasions! By what language can we sufficiently stigmatize the base conduct of a priesthood which will practice such outrageous fraud on an ignorant and confiding people!

From the splendid chapel which takes its name from that old rag, and where but few save the ragged were present, we went to the Waldensian chapel, of which the Rev. Mr. Bert is pastor. We had previously formed an acquaintance at the table of our chargé with this excellent and interesting man. His chapel is built in the centre of a square surrounded on all sides by houses, and which is entered by a large gateway. It is perfectly plain, externally and internally. The pulpit is high, with a sounding-board. The pews are made of benches, and texts of Scripture in large letters are written on all the walls, and meet the eye wherever it turns. O how strongly this contrasted with the images, and pictures, and the Sudario we had just left! The minister, in gown and bands, entered the pulpit, read the Scriptures, and read a very short form of prayer, without any change of position, which was standing. They sung chants from a book in which the words and music were printed together, accompanied by a small organ. Save in the reading of a form of prayer at the opening, the entire service was conducted as in our Presbyterian churches. The people seemed mostly, from their dress, of the humbler class, yet they seemed intelligent and devout. Their attention was marked through the entire service.

And are these, said I, at the close of the service, the descendants of the Waldenses, who have kept the lamp of truth burning in these Alpine valleys from the remotest ages of Christianity? Are these simple people the children of the Vaudois, that bribery could not corrupt—that war could not exterminate—that persecution could not wean from the faith of Christ—and that, like their own Alps, have withstood the storms raised for their destruction? Yes, these plain rustic people are their descendants; and I felt that I was in the presence of a royal race! What a green oasis amid the desolate Sahara of Popery is that Waldensian church at Turin! Although I could but very imperfectly follow in the worship which was there performed in French, yet as it was the first Protestant service I had attended for weeks, it was to me like a river of water in the wilderness, like the shadow of a great rock in a weary land!

I sought from Pastor Bert minute information as to their doctrine, their discipline, and their present state. In doctrine and discipline they are essentially Presbyterian; maintaining the doctrines of grace, infant consecration, the parity of the clergy, and government by Church courts. And at no period of their recent history have they been as flourishing as at present. On one of the new and finest streets of the city they were making arrangements to put up a noble edifice for the worship of God, amid the most dire opposition of the priests. Their numbers and wealth are greatly increased by the persecutions of Lombardy, Rome, and Naples; and with a full liberty of worship and of preaching the truth as it is in Jesus, they have an open field, and are seeking to cultivate it. Turin is just the place on which to plant our lever for the elevation and regeneration of Italy. It is an Italian city; there full religious liberty is secured; and there is an ancient, apostolical, evangelical, uncorrupted Church, fully, compactly, strongly organized, and cemented by the blood of martyrs and the persecutions of ages. Were Napoleon Bonaparte now alive, and did it offer the same advantages as a military post which it now does as a religious, he would send fifty thousand men across the Alps to occupy it.

CHAPTER XXIX.

Departure from Turin.—Ascent of the Alps.—Changes in Vegetation.—A Stream from the Clouds.—Going down the Alps.—Our Fellow-travelers: their Testimony as to Rome.—Chambéry.—Les Charmettes.—Priests abound.—Holy Hill.—Praying in a Hurry.—To Geneva.—First View.—Obvious Difference.—Friends in a far Country.

We took our departure from Turin with the most pleasant impressions as to the city, the government, and the people. The priests were fewer than we had met in any Italian city, which may partly account for the fact that we saw no beggars there. But there is no Sabbath there. The people are in form Papists; some go to mass in the morning—all ride or stroll about in the afternoon—and all places of amusement are open in the evening, which are usually thronged. Such is the effect of Popery every where. In a fine coach we were soon beyond the city lines, and on the magnificent road to Chambéry, along which on either side flowed a little streamlet for the purposes of irrigation. The city was behind us—the Superga, a church crowning the highest point of the Collina, and in which the royal family is buried, was on one side of us; and the Alps, with their snow-clad summits, formed a crescent before us. The air was hot—the valley was laden with a rich harvest; the hay and the grain was every where in the process of collection, and yet the snows of winter glittered upon all the mountains! As we entered the gorges of the Alps, the scenery became bold and grand beyond description; the air became cool, then cold, then colder, and by twelve at night we breathed the air of December, and in the region of eternal snows! What a transition in the brief space of about six hours! We ascended the steep mountains, over which, when viewed from below, it would seem impossible for a bird to fly, by a cork-screw road of astonishing formation, up which the horses trotted all the way! We passed from a mid-summer to a mid-winter climate, witnessing the corresponding changes of vegetation all the way. On the plains of the Po they were collecting a rich harvest. Soon we saw the grain in the green ear—soon in the blade, and higher up the farmer was planting. Soon the grape gave way to the pine of stunted growth, and soon every thing gave way to the barren rock and to eternal snow. The moon was full and cloudless, and so brilliant was its shining, that through all the watches of the night we could see

"Hills o'er hills, and Alps o'er Alps arise."

As we turned a certain curve in the road there towered a hill, at least a thousand feet above us, and from its very summit there came dashing a stream of water, which floated in the air like a ribbon for a little space, then was lost to the eye in mist or spray, then, touching a projecting part of the rock, it condensed again into a stream, and came foaming across our way! My friend was sleeping by my side. When this sight suddenly opened on us, I gave him a rouser with my elbow. He seemed not to relish the interruption of his repose; but when I pointed him to the cause of my sudden assault upon his ribs, with a most emphatic exclamation, " See there!" he was satisfied. I can assure my readers that I slept not a moment on the night we crossed Mount Cenis.

As the day began to dawn, which must have been about three o'clock, we passed the summit level, and commenced descending from our eagle height. As there was a strong opposition on the road, the driving was furious; and we thundered down the Alps with astonishing rapidity. Soon we reached the culture of April—soon the verdure of May and June; soon we saw the vine covering all the hills—soon we came to harvest-fields, such as we had left on the Po; and when we drove into the streets of Chambéry amid branches of green trees scattered over the streets, and adorning all the houses, marking a fête-day of Popery, the thermometer was again at 85°.

In this ride across the Alps, we had as our companions a Prussian countess and her maid of honor, both remarkably intelligent, and on their return from quite a sojourn in Rome. They were frank and communicative, and told us many things to illustrate the piety and purity of Romish priests. A few days after they entered Rome they were visited by a priest, who begged from them five scudi to assist a very afflicted family! He was a padre notorious for thus sustaining himself and his indolent brethren by collecting money under false pretenses. And yet he was not unfrocked! They also told of the daughter of a most tyrannical father, who wrote a letter to one of the cardinals that she could not endure longer the conduct of her parent, and stating her strong desire to enter a nunnery. In a few days the father died by poison. The daughter and a brother were arrested on suspicion; the letter was given in testimony against them, and they were found guilty of patricide; and the vast property of the father reverted to the priests! And it was the current belief that the priests poisoned the father! They also narrated a long story of a widow lady with whom they were on familiar intercourse. On the death of her husband, she repaired to Rome to enjoy the opportunities of devotion and seclusion which, she thought, it presented; but was soon compelled to retire from it because of the shameful conduct of her father confessor. Unless all testimony of natives and sojourners is utterly false, the priests of Rome are sinners above all men that live on the earth.

Chambéry is the capital of Savoy, and although pleasant for situation, is a town of mean appearance. It has one good street, but the rest are dark, dirty, narrow, and sombre. Near this place, and on a pleasant hill commanding a fine view, is the country house of "Les Charmettes," once the residence of Madame de Warens and Rousseau. But as the day was hot, and as my dislike for the man almost borders on detestation, I declined a pilgrimage to his residence. Although containing but about ten thousand inhabitants, Chambéry has fourteen convents, a Jesuit college, and priests and nuns out of all proportion to the number of the people. Hence the dilapidated appearance of the place and the beggarly appearance of the people. Why is it that priests and beggars go together? On an eminence near the town is a building containing a dead Christ, and on the pleasant way ascending to it are several little shrines, each containing a picture of some scene in the suffering of Christ; and to all praying at these shrines and worshiping the picture in the building which surmounts the hill, the same indulgences are promised which are granted to those who visit the holy shrines at Jerusalem! And poor people in dozens are seen daily piously ascending the hill to earn indulgences, and going cheerfully down it to revelry and indulgence! I stood for some time before one of the convents to gaze upon the padres as they passed in and out. The day was warm, and the windows were up. I was especially struck with the appearance of a good-looking man wearing a priest's cap and robe, who with quick step walked up and down an entry, reading his missal with railway speed. I could hear his voice, and, when he came to the window, could see his lips move. I never saw a man in such a hurry to get through his vespers. As it was about six in the evening, it was these he must have been repeating. And although in such a pressing hurry to end the formulary, he would stop and measure us with his black eye, but ceased not the utterance of his pater nosters. He seemed in as much hurry as if he had earned an indulgence, and desired to be away to practice it. Unless his eye and Burgundy face bore false witness against him, he could sin and pray with equal rapidity.

We spent a night in Chambéry, and were off for Geneva in the morning, accompanied by our Prussian countess, between whom and one of our party there sprung up quite a social and agreeable intercourse. We passed a finely cultivated valley to Aix-la-Bains, a celebrated bathing establishment. Thence we proceeded through Annecy, where lie the holy relics of St. Francis de Sales, to Geneva. The whole ride is a very fine one, through a very highly cultivated country, and rich in historical reminiscences. From Chambéry to Geneva you are at no time out of sight of the snowy Alps. About four P. M. we reached the summit of the hill, whence we had the first view of the lake, and of the city of Geneva. The sun shone brightly, the air was clear, and they lay in loveliness beneath us. Soon we passed the line which separates the kingdom of Sardinia and the canton of Geneva—a Papal and Protestant state—and were in Switzerland proper. The change in the appearance of the people was instantaneous. The moment you pass the gate you feel that you are in a Protestant country. You leave the beggars on one side of it; you meet a well-clad, industrious, and self-sustaining people on the other. Villas, increasing in sumptuousness and beauty, multiplied as we approached the city. Soon we entered its walls—for even Geneva is strongly fortified—and were rolled through clean streets filled with an active, industrious people, to the Hôtel de la Couronne, which is upon the lake, and overlooks its beautiful waters. We were now out of Italy, where reigns the very midnight of Popery, and in a free Protestant city, for centuries the bulwark of civil and religious liberty, and sacred to multitudes in all the earth, because of its association with the great Calvin, who was to the Reformers what Paul was to the Apostles, the most intellectual, and best educated of them all. Here we soon were in the embraces of dear Christian friends and acquaintances, from some of whom we separated in London, from others in Paris, and some of whom, on their return from the East, we first met here, making a most intelligent and agreeable American party. And it was pleasant to talk and laugh again in English, and in our own mother tongue to tell of our travels and adventures. We began again to enjoy the luxury of a home feeling.

CHAPTER XXX.

Geneva: its Attractions.—Miniature of Mont Blanc.—Missionary Anniversary.—The Oratoire.—A Drive up the Lake.—Ferney.—Voltaire.—Magnificent View.—A Soirée.—Dr. Malan.—D'Aubigné.—Gaussen.—La Harpe.—St. George.—Talk through an Interpreter.—Polite Interchange.—Love-feasts.

GENEVA has been many times described by travelers. Its great history and enchanting locality are sufficient to inspire dullness itself to try its hand at painting. It is on the southwest extremity of the Lake of Geneva, where the Rhone shoots out from the lake, dividing the city into two parts. These parts are united by bridges, so constructed as to add greatly to the beauty of the scene. The town is chiefly built on the left bank of the river, and rises gradually from the banks of the lake and river, so as to present a most beautiful appearance from the water. The streets are mostly narrow, and often very steep, and in the more elevated parts of the city there are many very fine residences. But the great attractions of the place lie in its history, and in its extended and beautiful environs.

Our first day in the city of Calvin was a very busy one, and was spent in a very miscellaneous way. A model of Mont Blanc was placarded all over the city for exhibition! We went to see it—like fools. We might as well have gone to see a cup of salt water as a specimen of the ocean! There Mont Blanc lay upon a table, and we could have secured a cabinet edition to carry to America! Thence we went to the Oratoire, the church where the theological professors, D'Aubigné, Gaussen, La Harpe, and others worship, to attend the anniversary of the Society for Missions. We saw there most of the evangelical pastors of the city and vicinity. Every thing was simple — ministers without gowns—extempore prayer — singing without instrumental music — pews like the seats in our lecture-rooms — and a pulpit with a small sounding-board. The church is on one of the highest points of the city—difficult of access to strangers who crowd the hotels on the lake, and in a position which would not attract a New York audience, which considers a fine church, on a fine street, and easy of access, as absolutely necessary to acceptable worship. At about six in the afternoon we crossed the bridge under which the "arrowy Rhone," here of indigo color, shoots from the lake, and drove up its bank in the direction of Ferney. Ever since the perusal of Macaulay's review of Frederick the Great, I have held Voltaire in the most sovereign contempt, and would not go a rod to visit his residence, which I saw in the distance. I gave my reasons to my companions, which were deemed satisfactory. We ascended a hill to witness the effect of the setting sun upon the surrounding scenery. The Jura range was on the west, over which a bright and cloudless sun hung suspended. Lake Lehman lay in beauty beneath us; on its opposite banks were villas and vineyards rising one above another in beautiful perspective; and skirting the distant horizon rose the fleecy Mont Blanc, piercing the heavens with its sharp and broken points. Although fifty miles in the distance, it seemed as just on the opposite side of the lake! As the sun declined, a blush appeared upon its pale, cold visage—that blush deepened every moment; and when the sun fell behind the Jura, the whole snowy range of Mont Blanc seemed in a blaze of fire. As the twilight came along, bringing night in its train, those distant fires died away as gradually as they were kindled, and "the monarch of mountains" looked down upon us as coldly as ever. No such magnificent view do I ever expect to take again. Our guide informed us that there are not ten days in the year on which the sight is seen to such perfection as we saw it. The effect upon us all was enchanting. We would say to every traveler, if necessary, wait a month at Geneva to see this sight.

We returned from this scene to one of a very different character, but yet equally gratifying to our feelings and tastes—a soirée, got up by the Missionary Society whose anniversary we attended in the afternoon. It was held in a hall provided for the purpose, and was fully attended. There was Dr. Malan, thin, of medium height, brisk in appearance, frank, and social, with hair white as Alpine snows flowing over his shoulders. And there was Dr. Merle d'Aubigné, large and full in stature, with heavy countenance, reserved, rather patronizing in his air, more English than French in his whole appearance, and seemingly impressed with the idea that he is rather a lion than otherwise. And there was Professor Gaussen, of middle stature, full habit, pleasant manners, silver gray, with a round French face. And there was Professor La Harpe, youthful, manly in all his developments, with a plump red and white cheek, more suggestive of "the sweetest isle of the ocean" than of the loveliest lake in the world. And there was Count de Saint George, tall, thin, youthful in appearance, bland in his manners, with rather a wealthy and aristocratic air, but by no means up to the offensive point. These were among the notables present. Ladies were there, ministering spirits, in large numbers. After the process of serving tea was ended, a psalm was sung with much spirit, the Scriptures were read, and prayer was offered, during which all stood. The plan was to have a brief address from some one from each of the countries there represented; and when the Americans were called on, they were so kind, or unkind, as to send me forth as their representative. I made a talk for about ten minutes, and was interpreted by a gentleman of the company—the first time I ever spoke to an assembly through an interpreter, nor shall I be sorry should it be my last. Although I knew not what I had said when I sat down, I was soon brought to my feet again by an address from the chair, thanking me in behalf of the meeting for my interesting and eloquent address on the occasion. Half suspecting that it might be a bit of French politeness, which sometimes induces to put the more abundant honor on the part that lacketh, I utterly declined to accept of their thanks on the grounds on which they were offered, stating that if any thing eloquent or worthy of their attention was uttered, it was interlarded by my interpreter, and that I would therefore hand [illegible] the thanks to him. If making fun at my expense, I determined that they should not have it all to themselves.

Soon after this passage at small arms the assembly dissolved itself into a Committee of the Whole, when we were introduced to gentlemen and ladies from the different cantons of Switzerland, from Germany, France, Italy, and Britain. Captain Packenham, the true-hearted Christian, exiled from Rome, where he was once a banker for the circulation of the Scriptures, was there, and gave a most interesting account of the good work of reformation in progress in Florence. On the whole, I was greatly gratified with this evening's entertainment. It was pleasant, social, cheerful, and yet pervaded by a truly religious spirit. They have a way of doing things in this manner in Britain, and here and there on the Continent, which might be introduced into our own country with happy effect. Their "breakfasts" in London, Edinburgh, Belfast, and Dublin accomplish much good. Meeting at a tea-table for an hour before a religious anniversary, where the speakers are introduced, compare notes, imbibe each other's spirit, so as to go out on the platform with a common feeling, and an acquaintance formed at a social repast, would relieve the dullness of many a May meeting in New York, and would greatly tend to cement Christians of various names together. These are "love-feasts" that might be safely and profitably introduced among us. The tea-drinking in a room in Exeter Hall, which preceded the meeting of the London Tract Society, where noble men representing the different branches of the Church spent an hour in pleasant social intercourse, I will never forget—as I can never forget the soirée in Geneva.

We returned to our lodgings at about eleven o'clock

in the evening, greatly gratified with our first day spent in Geneva. We all regretted that D'Aubigné did not sustain the impressions made on us by his noble History of the Reformation. If we act toward him, when he visits America, as he did toward the company of American clergy at that soirée, he will write us down as boors. He is getting up some fame for his incivilities, especially toward Americans. His History of the Reformation has given him a wide reputation, and, to save himself from the annoyances which are the tax of fame, he should not turn clown.

CHAPTER XXXI.

For Chamouny.—Enter Sardinia.—Obvious Change.—Fête at Bonneville. — The Ravine. — Fall d'Arpenaz.— Bridge at St. Martin's: its View.— Selling Echoes.— Ascent of Montanvert.— Mer de Glace.—Cracks in the Ice.—View from the Cottage.—Snow-balling.—Salanche.—Return to Geneva.

After an early breakfast we started, nine strong, and all from America, for Chamouny, a word which, however spelled, means always the same place. The world has but one Chamouny. In two carriages we soon passed the gates of the city, rode rapidly through the pleasant environs beyond, and at the distance of a few miles crossed a little stream which separates Geneva from Sardinia—an ancient Protestant republic from an ancient Papal kingdom. The change in the people was again observable, as when we entered Geneva from Sardinia. Soon we were met by beggars in all stages of rags and mutilation, and only got rid of them on our return to the city of Calvin. The day was balmy and cloudless. We observed by the idleness of the people—their standing in groups here and there—and by the branches of trees standing against houses, and suspended from windows—that something was going on. As we approached Bonneville, the road was thick with people crowding to the old town. It was a fête day of Popery, but in honor of what god or goddess I could not learn. We stopped to dine, and to witness the gay and utterly ridiculous pageant

At the ringing of a bell a procession commenced moving from the village church. It was headed by women in white robes. These were followed by children, neatly dressed, bearing baskets of rose-leaves; these by children bearing censers; these by priests fat and well-fed; these by a large, ruby-faced bishop, bearing the host under a splendid canopy: behind the canopy marched the civil officers of the place, who were followed by a vast concourse of people. It was now midday, and the sun was hot, and the road very dusty. At certain signs the whole mass of the people knelt in the dust—rose again—turned to the right or left—halted or marched. The master of ceremonies sounded a whistle, and the boys scattered leaves for the priests and bishop to walk on, or they turned round and offered incense to the bishop and host. The soldiers were present in great numbers, and in full uniform, and saluted the host with volleys of musketry as it approached. And when the bishop stopped, as he frequently did, and turned round the host so as to face the soldiers, they all fell instantly on their knees, save the officers, who leaned on their swords with their faces to the earth. After parading the streets in this way for some time, the bishop and priests returned to the church, and the people and soldiers went to drink and to play. When the exhibition was over the streets were full of revelry. And with such mountebank exhibitions as these, gotten up by the priests to delude the people, the Papal world is full. And belief in this, and all its kindred nonsense, is what the priests call faith in God!

Thoroughly disgusted with this priestly ceremony,

we resumed our journey, and after crossing the Arve several times on noble bridges, and passing through some towns of but little note, we entered a defile beneath towering, and often overhanging precipices, which mark the first grand entrance into the great Alpine ravine. And now our road lay on the banks of the Arve, which flows between mountains often 8000 feet high, and sometimes rising from either bank like walls! Soon the waterfall D'Arpenaz, the highest in Savoy, rose to view, which, like that seen crossing Mont Cenis from Turin, leaps out from the very summit of the mountain, is broken into spray and lost to the sight; condenses on the rocks below, and rushes under a bridge into the Arve. It forms an object of great beauty. Beyond this jeu d'eau, the valley widens, and rich fields spread up the sides of the snow-capped mountains to Salanche. Here is a bridge crossing the Arve, on one side of which is the dirty town of St. Martin, and on the other the not very magnificent one of Salanche; and from that bridge we caught our first near view of Mont Blanc, and the one that most deeply impressed us. In looking up the valley, beyond the wintery bed of the Arve, rises the mountain of Forclaz, its sides clothed with pine, and its summit with pasturage. Above that rises the Aiguille de Gouté, and the Dome de Gouté, white as can be. And yet beyond and above these, Mont Blanc towers to the clouds, presenting a sight worth a voyage round the world to see! It is here every feeling of your soul responds to the glorious description of the poet:

"Mont Blanc is the monarch of mountains;
They crown'd him long ago,"

> On a throne of rocks, in a robe of clouds,
> With a diadem of snow."

What a pity Coleridge did not date his immortal hymn at this bridge, instead of in the vale of Chamouny, where the "monarch" is entirely hid from view!

Here we left our carriages for that vehicle peculiar to this mountain country, called *char-à-banc*, in which we pursued our course to the vale along a gorge wondrous all the way. We never left the sound of the dashing Arve, nor the sight of snow and rich verdure! At a turn in the road where a high bridge is crossed, and where all travelers have to work their passage up a very steep hill, we were surrounded by boys who wished to sell us some echoes. One would shoot a gun, and you would hear it cracking off many times among the hills. Another would sound his horn, and the mountains promptly and repeatedly replied. And then, hat or cap in hand, they would most resolutely importune you. Not knowing how to get rid of them, and not willing to encourage vagrants, against whom guide-books and travelers warn you, I ascended a hill, and after a full inflating of my lungs, let go a shout which woke up all the mountains. The boys stood aghast, and pushing my advantage, I took off my hat and commenced begging them in turn! They were completely routed, and followed us no farther. They found I could make my own echoes, and had no need to buy any. We reached the vale before ten o'clock at night, shivering with cold, although, judging from our feelings, the thermometer must have been 85° during the afternoon.

We made all our preparations for an early ascent of

Montanvert. We arranged as to our mules and guides on our arrival, and as the former were rather scarce, myself and a friend agreed to take one between us. This I liked very well when it was my turn to ride; but when I had to walk, I resolved most firmly to have a mule to myself the next time I went up that steep path. Through all kinds of paths but pleasant ones—picking our way amid rocks and stones—now crossing the pathway of the avalanche—now threading a cork-screw path up a steep spot—now sheltered by pines—now passing through a pasturage of sheep, and now passing through snow-banks rising six feet high on either hand, we finally gained the cottage on the summit of the mountain. It was wonderful to see the dexterity and unerring accuracy of the mules through every step of the way. Not once did they stumble or tread upon a loose stone. We descended on the other side of the cottage to the far-famed "Mer de Glace." This is a ravine winding among the mountains for many leagues, and filled with ice at some points three hundred feet thick! We crossed this enormous sea of ice nearly to the opposite mountain; we kneeled by its enormous cracks and looked down through them into the profound depths, and could hear the glacier torrent battling its way at the bottom. A man once fell into one of these cracks, whose body no effort could recover. Many years afterward, as we were told by the guides, a boy fell into the same crack, and in fishing for the boy they drew up the man, and so undecayed that his friends could recognize him! His body was so frozen as to prevent the process of corruption. The view from Montanvert is wild and grand beyond description.

Beneath is the vale of Chamouny, reposing in beauty, beyond which rises the Flégère, robed in white ; on the other side of you lies the Mer de Glace, one of the wonders of the world ; and beyond and around it rise those Alpine needles called Aiguille du Dru, Aiguille du Moine, and the Aiguille Vert, which is 13,000 feet above the level of the ocean, and which stretches up before you toward the stars 7000 feet from the place where you are standing. Behind those needles, and concealed by them from our view, Mont Blanc reposed in serene majesty, lifting its sky-pointing peaks nearer than any of them toward the throne of its glorious Creator.

It was enough. After feasting our eyes upon the wild grandeur by which we were surrounded, we commenced our descent, partly on foot, partly on our mules. And that we might be enabled to tell of it to our friends, myself and two ladies had a regular snow-balling on the 21st day of June, on our return to the vale below.

We returned to Salanche in the evening, where, with Mont Blanc in full view from our window, and surrounded with other peaks clothed in snow, we spent a pleasant night. After an early breakfast, we resumed our carriages on our return to Geneva, feeling that we had seen sights which, beyond any that we had ever seen, display the greatness, the glory, the omnipotence of Jehovah.

CHAPTER XXXII.

Geneva: its Influence.—Calvin: his System.—Knox.—Sunday in Geneva.—The Market-place.—St. Peter's.—Gaussen in the Oratoire.—Cathedral Services.—Dr. Malan's Chapel.—An Evening with his Family.—Sabbath Desecration.—Importance of rightly sanctifying the Sabbath.—To whom we owe its true Keeping.

We returned from Mont Blanc for the purpose of spending a Sabbath in the city of Calvin, and of seeing more of its sights. Small as is the town, and secluded as it is between the Jura and the Alps, its political influence upon Europe, and its religious influence upon the world, have been vast. Right or wrong, John Calvin, who found here a home and a grave, was a great man. In proof of this we present his Institutes, which, considering he was educated a Papist, and for the bar, and that they were published while he was yet under thirty years of age, form an enduring monument to his memory. In profound thought, in scriptural knowledge, in acute discrimination, in severe analysis, in close logical processes, where or by whom have they been surpassed? We are no advocates for the religious or political errors of Calvin; he himself taught strongly the doctrine of human fallibility—those called by his name can afford to confess that in some things he erred; but his most bitter opponents must grant to him a most powerful and far-reaching intellect. And because founded on Scripture and reason, his doctrines and polity have undergone less change, and now need less mending than do those of any other branch of the Church of the Reformation. You are shown the house in which he lived, and in which he died; but the spot of his burial, like that of Moses, is unknown. The severity he exercised toward others he practiced toward himself, and carried out as to his own memory. Wishing no pilgrimages to his grave by future generations, he forbade the Genevese to mark his grave in any way. His monument is the system of truth which he unfolded, and which it is far easier to calumniate than to confute. To him, more perhaps than to any other man, are we indebted for those most important and glorious institutions, "*a Church without a bishop, and a state without a king*." The services he rendered in these directions to the world make a great atonement for his severity and errors.

Here too it was, and under the teachings of Calvin, that John Knox, an exile for the truth, lit his lamp—the lamp which illumined Scotland, which, in a religious point of view, is the glory of all lands.

The Sabbath sun rose beautifully over the Alps, and shone warmly and without a cloud upon the lake, the city, and the Jura Mountains. We went at ten o'clock to the Oratoire, but the services were just ending as we reached it, having commenced at the early hour of eight o'clock. In our way we passed through the great market-place, which was thronged with peasants from the country, in a rustic and peculiar garb, every one bearing a stick laced to his back, and extending about a foot above his head. They stood in rows like soldiers, and neither moved nor conversed. After some inquiry, I learned that they were mowers from the surrounding country, who came there to be hired, as it was now the season for cutting hay; and they stood in the market-place ready to be hired. On our return from church we passed through the same market-place, and found but few of them left. The stick laced to their back was the handle of their scythes.

We repaired to the Cathedral of St. Peter's, one of the most conspicuous objects of the city. It is simple in its architecture, very capacious, and contains few objects worthy of interest. It was here Calvin preached with such power and effect, that profligacy was compelled to hide its head. It is now in the possession of the Church of the Canton, and its preachers are Unitarian. The place was chilly, although the day was hot; benches for pews, but few in attendance; not a person occupied the fine seats prepared for the city authorities, opposite the pulpit: there was an organ at one end of the building, and a chorister under the pulpit. The preacher seemed remarkably animated and fluent, and used no notes. The people seemed uninterested. There was nothing to interest us in the service, nor in the people, nor in the place, save that Calvin and his companions uttered truths within these walls which made, and still make, Rome tremble, and which will live forever. Thence we returned to the Oratoire, and spent a most interesting hour in hearing Dr. Gaussen instructing a very large congregation of young people in the Bible by way of question and answer. To us it was gratifying to see so few in the Cathedral listening to the errors of Socinianism, and to see the Oratoire so crowded, and with the young, where the simple truth as it is in Jesus is so faithfully proclaimed.

I know not why nor how it is, but Cathedral worship is substantially the same every where. Whether performed at St. Peter's or St. John Lateran, at Rome; or at St. Paul's or Westminster Abbey, in London; or at St. Peter's, in Geneva; or in the old Cathedral in Glasgow, it is the same cold, formal, drawling service, which neither stimulates the mind nor warms the heart. And they seem every where alike deserted, by Papists, Episcopalians, and Presbyterians, save when some novelty attracts a crowd. We learn that even at old Trinity, in New York, the audience at matins and vespers is often not more than twice as large, deducting officials, as was that of Dean Swift's, when reduced to "dearly beloved Roger." The world will not be much the loser when drawling Cathedral services of every kind shall come to a perpetual end. They were instituted in days of darkness by indolent priests, for an ignorant people. We know not a solitary benefit they confer on the race, while they do much to sustain priestly arrogance and to perpetuate superstition.

At five P.M. we went, in company with two friends, to the chapel of the Rev. Dr. Malan. It is a small building within the inclosure of his own premises, and of the very plainest construction. And small as it is, it was not crowded. Over its door is this inscription, in French, "Jesus said unto those that loved him, My peace I leave unto you, my peace I give unto you." The service was in French, and in form like unto that which obtains in all Presbyterian churches. The manner of the doctor was solemn, but stiff; and his utterance was fluent and vivacious. On his kind invitation, we spent the evening with his family, and a charming family it is, all of them speaking English most fluently. In an interview with him under his magnificent elms, I learned from him that he held connection neither with the state nor the evangelical party. The state party he considers corrupt to the core, and the evangelical party as far too lax in doctrine and discipline. "I am," said he, "a Princeton man, and I can not unite with the evangelical party in many things." And on learning that I was educated in Princeton, and that my mind was first arrested to the consideration of religious things by the preaching of Dr. John M. Mason, of New York, no longer able to contain his feelings, he most lovingly embraced me.

After tea was served, the family was collected for worship. One played upon the piano, and all sung. He himself led in prayer, in French, until he came to invoke God's blessings upon his guests, and their country, and friends, when he at once used the English. When supplication on our behalf was concluded, he resumed the French. The whole service was unique and altogether delightful. When prayers were ended we all drew round a centre-table, on which was placed a basket with slips of paper, on which were written texts of Scripture as mottoes. Each person, in their turn, drew a slip from the basket, and the text it contained was explained with some reference to the person drawing it. This was, for at least an hour, a source of amusement, interest, and instruction. And the whole was ended by each person around the table making some contribution to the cause of missions. A more sweet, Christian, simple, cultivated family we have never met. As we retired from the lovely circle never more, probably, to see the venerable patriarch who presides over it, we could forgive the sentence painted over his door, and which first offended, because seemingly too ostentatious: "*Mais pour moi et ma maison nous servirons l'Eternel;*" as for me and my house, we will serve the Lord.

Because of the large infusion of a Popish population, and of the proverbially lax views of the Continental reformers as to the Lord's day, the Sabbath is sadly desecrated in Geneva. They were erecting, vis-a-vis to our hotel on the right bank of the Rhone, a very large building, to accommodate the throngs brought together by their periodical shooting-match, where the cantons are all represented by their best marksmen. And from the dawning of the Sabbath's sun to its setting, they were working on the building, and in every direction they were practicing on the rifle. We have already described the scene witnessed in the market-place. The shops were every where open, and people were buying and selling. My friend took a walk through some of the fashionable promenades, and outside the walls of the city, during the evening, and he testifies that he witnessed no Sabbath desecration in Paris to surpass that of Geneva, especially beyond the walls. Mortified with Parisian laxness where we expected Scotch or New England strictness in the observance of the Lord's day, we made inquiry as to its cause, and we were informed that Calvin himself, for the purpose of bearing testimony against Judaizing views of the Sabbath, would often go through the markets and stores of the city, making purchases as on any other day of the week! Having heard this, and learning that the evangelical clergy of the city entertained the lax views of Calvin, we could account for the Sabbath desecration on all sides visible around us.

While there is a narrow and ceremonial view of the Sabbath, which makes it a day of gloom instead of the "pearl of days," there is also a lax view of it, which tends to make it more a day of pleasure than of devotion. And it is very remarkable to what a degree the maintenance, and the transmission from one generation to another, of pure, and simple, and spiritual Christianity, are connected with the true sanctification of the Sabbath day. We owe its sanctification, under God, not to Luther, or Calvin, or to the Continental reformers, but to English Puritans and Scotch Presbyterians. And we owe to these many other things which are now blessing the Church and the world.

CHAPTER XXXIII.

Up Lake Lehman.—Lausanne.—Farrel.—Priestly Profligacy.—Captain Packenham.—His Definition.—Neufchatel.—Needed Reformation.—Farrel's Visit.—His Grave.—To Basle: its Appearance—its History—its Reformation.—Œcolampadius.—Erasmus.

At nine o'clock in the morning the "Aigle" turned her prow up Lake Lehman, and in a short time Geneva faded away from our view. We gazed upon it, beautiful for situation, until we could see it no more. The lake was quiet as a sleeping child; it rained heavily, and straight from above; and the Alps and the Jura Mountains, on our right and left, were robed in clouds. On a clear day this is a sail of great beauty. Before reaching Lausanne, the rain ceased, the clouds soon passed away, and the capital of the Canton de Vaud rose beautifully on our view.

Lausanne lies on the slope of a hill, which rises gradually from the lake, and at the distance of about two miles from the place of landing. It is intersected by several deep ravines, giving it the appearance of distinct villages. The streets are up and down, and some of them so steep as to be utterly impassable by carriages. But from some of the high points, as from the terrace of the old Cathedral, the view of the city, the lake, the distant Alps, is very fine. Cooper, our greatest American novelist, says of a point above this city, that "it offers one of the grandest landscapes of this noblest of earthly regions." You are shown the house in which Gibbon concluded his history of the Decline and Fall of the Roman Empire, the writing of which was first suggested amid the magnificent ruins of the Coliseum. This city was the residence of Haller, Tissot, Voltaire, and Gibbon; it possesses at this day a most refined society, and is yet the resort of many foreigners for the education of their children. Here Farrel and other Reformers displayed great energy and eloquence in the promotion of the great work of the Reformation. It is said that in no part of Europe was the conduct of the priests so utterly shameless as here. They would often issue in companies from the bishop's palace, and from the religious houses, drunk, armed with rapiers and swords; would murder men and women in the riots that would ensue; and after indulgence in all kinds of brutal licentiousness, would return to mass, the missal, and the confessional, where they would mutually confess, and then absolve one another! The city was under the care of Mary, but Venus was the divinity of the priests. The episcopal palace is yet standing, faded, and deserted by priests and their prostitutes; but as you gaze upon it, the remembrance of other days comes over you, and the prayer involuntarily rises from your heart, that the Papal banner may never again float from its turrets, and that the war-cry of Sebastian may never again go forth from its halls.

We here met again the warm, generous, Christian, and self-sacrificing Captain Packenham, the exile from Rome and Tuscany because of his efforts to circulate the Scriptures. He is an Irishman by birth. He was an officer in the British navy, and he has lived in Italy until familiar as a native with its language and institutions. "What," said I to him, "is your honest estimate of the Catholic priests of the Continent?" I never will forget the emphasis and the energy of his reply. "*Popery and its priests are simply and only the police of despotism.*" This definition should be hung up where the nations should read it. To all Americans I would say, "Keep it before the people!"

The fine country between Lausanne and Neufchatel we traversed at night in a diligence, and reached the latter city in the early morning. It lies upon a steep slope of the Jura Mountains, and is famed for its manufacture of poor Burgundy, poor watches, and poor jewelry. And to these poor things I would add, from personal experience, poor hotels and poor fare. The town seems neither Swiss, French, nor German; but a mixture of them all, and not of the best elements of either; a kind of patois is spoken, which retains the barbaric, and drops the refined.

But here was a reformation work of surpassing interest. In that old Cathedral canons of the most depraved character said mass; and in that building above the town, whose ruins are shown you, the monks of Fontaine-André prayed and reveled. The canons and monks were at open war. Both were equally wicked. They kept their mistresses—clothed them sumptuously—endowed their children—fought in the church—haunted the streets by night; and, to gratify their lusts, plundered the people. One day a frail boat was seen crossing the lake, from which was landed a small, thin, pale man, with sun-burned complexion, red beard, sparkling eyes, expressive mouth, his every feature expressive of an iron will. It was Farrel. The canons and monks would have hailed a hundred plagues in preference to him. Forbidden admission to all churches, he mounted a stone, which is yet shown the traveler, and preached to the people. The canons and monks made a vigorous defense. Their shaven crowns were seen every where in the crowd; they supplicated, menaced, threatened, howled; but it was useless. They sought to blast his character—then to murder him; but it was all over with them. The people of Neufchatel received the word of God. And as the sun was rising over the Alps, and over the lake, at one end of which this city lies, I was treading the ground on which Farrel preached, and viewing the old Cathedral where the canons carried on their orgies—on the terrace of which Farrel was buried, and in which the doctrines of the Reformation are now preached. If Geneva is the city of Calvin, Neufchatel is the city of Farrel. Its historic glory is not in its princes of the house of Chalons, nor in its subjection to Marshal Berthier, nor yet to the house of Brandenburg, but to its having received the Gospel, "as if it had but one soul," from Farrel. Like the grave of Calvin, there is no stone to point out the precise spot where his mortal is waiting the call to put on its immortality.

The ride from Neufchatel to Basle is one of great beauty at points. The road lies on the shores of lakes Neufchatel and Bienne; for several miles the waters are on one side, and the slopes and spurs of the Jura, clad with vines to their very summits, on the other. We crossed a low ridge of the Jura by a very fine road, and soon we struck a stream, which is one of the many which forms the head waters of the Rhine. Then we commenced a descent, which continued for hours, down a road which followed this stream, and through a defile of fearful grandeur. It would seem as if the entire gorge, with its steep banks, must have been the result of human labor and gunpowder; but that awful ravine, and the walls of solid rock, that tower to heaven on either side, are the work of the great Architect. As we emerged from it, the ruins of old fortifications, which date back to the days of Cæsar, were on either hand, and a beautiful plain opened before us, over which we galloped until we passed the walls and entered the old city of Basle. Although yet in Switzerland politically, we were now fairly out of it physically. And although bordering on Switzerland, Germany, and France, every traveler would say, on riding through Basle—on reading the signs over shops and the names on doors—on witnessing the dress of the females, with ribbons too long and dresses too short—on seeing the style of architecture, and the variegated painting of the houses, that it fairly belongs to the Dutch. None knowing the premises would say that this would be a violent inference.

Basle has a great history, although not a great place. It dates back to the fourth century; and because lying at the head of navigation on the Rhine, it became rich and powerful. During the Middle Ages it was governed by warlike bishops, whose conflicts with their brethren often devastated the surrounding country. In the fourteenth century it was first decimated by war; then ravaged by a plague, from which only three families escaped; and then was laid in ruins by an earthquake! It had so far recovered from this awful ruin as to be selected as the seat of the great Council which met there in 1431, which did so much for the moral reformation of the clergy, and which is therefore so much maligned by the holy, apostolical Church. Would it not be well for those who tell us of the unity and infallibility of the Papal Church to read again the very edifying history of this Council of Basle? And there yet stands the old Cathedral in which that Council sat, now happily consecrated to the preaching of the Gospel.

It was here the work of reformation, blended with that of revolution; and although the excitement was intense, the mass was exchanged for the Gospel without the shedding of a drop of blood. The people took the work of reform into their own hands; they entered the churches, tore down their idols, and burned them in the street on Ash-Wednesday. "The idols," said the wags, "are keeping their Ash-Wednesday to-day!" "I am surprised," said Erasmus, "that they perform no miracle to save themselves: formerly the saints worked prodigies for much smaller offenses."

In the course of a few weeks, every thing was changed in this city. The Gospel was preached in all its churches, and the mass was pronounced an idolatrous rite the moment it was understood by the people. Œcolampadius was the great instrument in the hand of God of this change. And he stands to Basle in the relation in which Farrel stands to Neufchatel, and Calvin to Geneva.

Basle was the residence of the learned, the time-serving, the vain, the cowardly Erasmus, who favored the doctrines of the Reformation, and yet wrote against Luther; who scoffed at Popery, and yet was fretted at its overthrow. Here, also, is his grave. Here were born Œcolampadius, Wetstein, Buxtorf, the Bernouillis, and Euler. Here Zwingle was educated. Here Calvin, Arminius, De Watte, Oken, and others found refuge from persecution. And here is a missionary school, which has sent out over all the heathen world some of the most useful and faithful missionaries now laboring to gild the earth with the light of the Gospel. Many and noble are the recollections which cluster around the city of Basle.

CHAPTER XXXIV.

Departure from Basle.—Valley of the Rhine.—Variety of Travelers. —Characteristic Reply.—An Observer.—A Question answered.—Strasburg: its wondrous Clock.—Advice to the Priests.—The Cathedral.—An American Prelate.—Jews burned.—Why no Relics. —Poor Scotland.—Searched.—To Baden-Baden.

At an early hour in the morning we stepped into an omnibus, and were driven across the famous old bridge which connects Basle and *Little* Basle, and on which stood the grotesque figure, "Lallen König," which, by the movement of a pendulum, constantly protruded its tongue and rolled up its goggle eyes, making contemptuous faces at Little Basle. A ride of three miles through a rich bottom-land brought us to the railway station, and in a few minutes we were out of Switzerland, perhaps forever.

The railway keeps along, on what we would call the second bank of the Rhine, and for hours the river, and its wide, level, and fertile bottom-lands were in full view. There are no fences, and but few trees to obstruct the vision; and at a glance we could see hundreds of people, men and women, mostly women, making hay. The view was often picturesque. As in Italy, the women here work just as do men, and hire out in the same way for about twenty dollars a year. There is no kind of field service which they do not perform.

One meets abroad with every variety of travelers,

and especially from America. We are a locomotive people, loving travel beyond any other. Our men of tact and industry make money rapidly, and spend it often lavishly and unwisely. But few Europeans travel save scholars and the aristocracy; but Americans of every grade, if they have the means, will travel, unless kept at home by some strong antagonistic influence. Hence you meet with some of them in the Coliseum, utterly ignorant of its great history—and in St. Peter's, who see there nothing to admire—and paying a thousand francs for a modern daub, as a production of one of the great masters—and seeing nothing of art in the great frescoes of Angelo in the Sistine—and passing unnoticed the "Dying Gladiator." Hence the laughable and characteristic reply of an American merchant, on his return from Rome, when asked by a friend in Liverpool, "Well, sir, you have been in Rome, what do you think of it?" "Not very much, sir; I think its public buildings are very sadly out of repair!"

We had as fellow-traveler down the Rhine one of these sagacious Americans. He was a general, and an ex-state senator, and a brewer, according to his own showing. He was large enough for a general, pompous enough for a senator, and there was a swelling protuberance beneath his waistcoat which might suggest the idea that he had swallowed a barrel. He slept most soundly near me as we flew along our iron way. I greatly disliked to have him lose the points of great attraction which were rapidly opening upon us and as rapidly receding. We turned a curve where a beautiful panoramic view opened up, and laying my hand upon him, I gave him a hearty shake, exclaiming, "General, what a beautiful view!" He rubbed his eyes and looked out for a moment, and as he quietly composed himself for another sleep, he replied, "I passed up this way before." After that I gave him up. He was a fit subject for staying at home, and is a fit representative of a certain class of travelers. "Were you at Naples when abroad, sir?" said I to one of our upper ten. His reply was characteristic. "I really forget, sir," said he; and, turning to one of his daughters, he asked, "were we, Sarah?" "O yes," she blushingly replied; "do you not remember Vesuvius?" But all traces even of Vesuvius seemed buried under the lava of dollars and cents. Why do such persons travel?

To Strasburg from Basle, the country is very level, and you are rarely out of view of the Rhine. We stopped to see the famous Cathedral, whose immensely high tower is visible at a great distance. We crossed the river on a bridge of boats, the first we had ever seen, and which recalled the days of Cæsar. It seemed as firm as if made of wood or of stone. We met French soldiers and officers on the opposite bank, who ordered us out of our little carriage, and searched all its boxes, and felt over our persons in quest of contraband goods. Having none, they permitted us to pass on. We soon crossed the motes, and entered by the ponderous gates set in the prodigious fortifications which guard this border town; and as the hour of high noon was approaching, we drove with rapid pace to the chamber of the famous clock in the Cathedral.

This clock is a wonderful affair, standing as high,

if not higher, than our largest church organs. At twelve o'clock, Death comes out and strikes the hour. Then commences a series of wonders. The twelve apostles pass in review before the Savior, who stands over them with uplifted hands. And a rooster, made of brass, shakes his wings and crows thrice. If not perfect, the imitation is very fine. The noise of his brazen wings and feathers, when clapping them, was too ringing to be natural. And this clock tells not only the time of day, but the day of the week, the day of the month, the month of the year, the changes of the weather, the phases of the moon, the complicated movement of the planets; and, in addition, it plays several tunes and marches by way of pastime. This clock was constructed by Isaac Habrecht, in reference to whom many stories are told. It ran down, and got out of repair; and for years there was no mechanic that could repair it. Even Bonaparte took its repair into consideration. A man was finally found who could comprehend its wonderfully complicated machinery, and repair it. And we witnessed, with hundreds of others, its extraordinary evolutions at twelve o'clock at noon. As the Cathedral is in the possession of the Papists, it is a matter of wonder they do not make a saint out of Isaac Habrecht, and a standing miracle out of his astonishing mechanism. It seems to me the priests could make more out of it than out of the bungle of the blood of Januarius, or the winking Madonna of Rimini. I would advise them to try their hand at it. The only objection to the effort is the extreme tendency of the German mind to incredulity. Yet there are many of easy faith with whom they might succeed.

When ordered out of the chamber of the clock, we went through and round the great Cathedral. It has two towers and but one spire, and that the highest in the world—higher than the dome of St. Peter's, than Cheops, the highest pyramid of Egypt. The whole building is the most distinguished specimen of Gothic architecture in existence, and its tracery the finest in the world. After viewing this and the other sights of the city, we dined at one of the best ordered hotels we saw in Europe. It was here we met the pedantic little archbishop of Ohio, with a big cross before him, and a stupid-looking priest acting as lackey, behind him. We asked some of the waiters who he was, and if his reverence had only seen some of the grimaces which they made behind his back, he would have been not much more pleased than on his recent defeat on the school question in his own beloved Cincinnati. They were either very poor Papists, or Protestants no better than they ought to be. It requires as much brass to be a Popish priest now, even in some Papal countries, as it did to be an augur in the waning days of the superstition of the Roman empire.

Strasburg has its history. It was the Argentoratum of the Romans, and, because of its position, has been for centuries a commercial town of considerable importance. Here two thousand Jews were burned on the suspicion of having poisoned the wells and fountains of water! Here the art of printing was invented. Here the Reformation gained some of its earliest triumphs; and a great portion of the people are yet Lutherans. Here some terrible revolutionary scenes were enacted. Here the Marseillaise Hymn was written by De Lisle

Here Vauban, famous for his skill in erecting fortifications, earned many laurels. And yet all its lions are soon seen; and after that, there is nothing to induce a wish to tarry. I made some inquiry for relics in the Papal churches, but could not learn that there were any. Somehow or other, holy bones, coats, nails, and pieces of wood seem to hate Protestants as much as do the priests; and where there is a strong sprinkling of unbelievers as in Strasburg, the relics become bashful, and refuse to obtrude themselves! This may be the reason why they abound in Italy, while I know not that there is even the holy parings of a holy nail in Scotland! Poor Scotland!

Again we passed the gates of this old city and the Rhine; and on the Baden side we were examined by officers, just as we were on the French side when going over. These officials seemed to mistrust the ladies more than the men, and on that account pressed their clothes less tenderly, and scrutinized them more closely. But we were soon on the railway, and drew up at Baden-Baden about six o'clock in the evening, a town beautiful for situation, and noted as a watering-place. Although the season had scarcely commenced, the streets were full of people—most of them, like ourselves, strangers.

CHAPTER XXXV.

Baden-Baden.—Conversation House.—The Gambling-room.—The Manner of the Game, and Gamblers.—Monopoly in Gambling!—Hot Springs.—Their Manner of Use.—The new Castle.—Breakfast-room.—Underground Apartments.—Awful History.

After locating ourselves in the Hôtel d'Angleterre, we went forth in the cool of the evening to see Baden-Baden. Hill and vale, palace and cottage, splendor and poverty are mixed up together. So steep are some of the streets as to render them difficult of ascent on foot. A dense forest skirts the town, netted by beautiful walks, which adds greatly to the attractions of the place. Opposite to our hotel, and in the background of a large green, rose the Conversation House, devoted to the various purposes of balls, card parties, eating, drinking, smoking, and gambling. And we saw men and *women* engaged in these pursuits, even to the smoking and gambling!! Very large trees throw a dense shade over the part of the green in front of the house, and hundreds were sitting beneath them, of all ages and sexes, sipping wine, coffee, and ices, in great glee, and apparently very happy.

But the place which most attracted our attention here was the famous gambling-room, of which we had heard much, and which we resolved to see for ourselves.

This room is connected with the Conversation House, and is finely frescoed and furnished. There are no green blinds or curtains to conceal persons from view.

It is on the first floor, beautifully lighted, and exposed to public view. It is open to all—all may enter it, but all save those who venture are forbidden to take seats. We stood at least an hour to witness the operation, and to study human nature. Piles of gold and silver lay on the table, and by the elbows of a man called "the banker." A machine was there, which was turned rapidly round, out of which a small ball soon dropped upon a board below, which was squared; these squares were variously colored and numbered. And it would seem that whether the player won or lost was determined by the square and the number in which the ball reposed. As I did not understand the game, I commenced reading the gamblers. The "banker" uttered not one syllable during the time I stood there. He watched the ball, and, as he won or lost, threw out or raked in the gold or silver. There was no conversation above a whisper around the table. There was no appeal—no scolding. One man threw down a Napoleon: he lost it—then two—then three—then five: he lost them all, and retired obviously disappointed; but not a word did he utter. An old man threw down five gold pieces: he lost them, and retired. A man in mid life with jaunty air threw down three pieces; the banker paid over: three more he won again and again. He retired with cheerful countenance; and, as he retired, the leaden eye of the banker fell upon him; but not a word was uttered. Some women were seated at the table, with all the soul they had, both as to quality and quantity, in the game; but they did not play during our stay there. That they do play is notorious, and some of them even stake their virtue when their money is gone! But such must have lost their virtue before their money. The winner of such virtue gains a very doubtful prize.

This was such a sight as I had never previously witnessed. That cold-blooded banker, schooled in crime and in the art of deception, watching for victims as a spider for flies—passion rising and falling in his face as he won or lost, and as quietly as mercury in the thermometer; those victims throwing down their money in hope, losing it, and going away in despair; those women, with fingers sparkling with jewels, witnessing and abetting the whole. O, if I have ever seen fiends in human form, I believe it was round that swindling machine in Baden-Baden! And this gambling-house belongs to the Duke of Baden, who claims a monopoly in gambling, and who farms his monopoly to a company in Paris at an enormous yearly rent! How humiliating, that such robbers and blacklegs should rank among princes! This is a town beautiful for situation, but its moral atmosphere is contaminating.

The hot springs of Baden form its great attraction and curiosity. The main spring issues from the side of the mountain, which rises over the town, and which is surmounted by the palace of the reigning duke. Over this spring is erected a large building, in which is a large basin for the reception of the water, whose heat as it issues from the rock is 154 degrees. The steam that rises from it is conveyed into apartments for steam baths. The water is conveyed into others for hot baths, where it is cooled to the required point. From this reservoir it is conveyed in pipes over the whole town, and at every corner you see the people drawing hot water.

Indeed, it is conveyed across the river that flows through the town to a fine building called the Drink-hall, where people resort for the waters in the morning, as they do in Saratoga to the Congress Spring, and where it retains undiminished its heat and its virtues. The use of these waters is regulated by law, and none are permitted to bathe in them without an order from a physician. Unless the system is in a state to require them, bathing in them is greatly injurious. A single bath gave to a traveling friend a pair of black eyes, from which he did not recover for weeks. One cup at the Drink-hall fully satisfied us. The water smells like poor broth, and has a salty, alkalish taste.

We made a morning call at the new castle of the duke, which surmounts the hill, and were shown through all its apartments. As if for our accommodation, he had just retired from his breakfast-room, that we might see the table at which a reigning prince sipped coffee. We have seen the breakfast room and table of many in America more richly furnished. The upper apartments wore quite an air of poverty, after having seen those of Versailles, the Quirinal, and Turin. But the underground apartments possess a fearful interest. With lighted torches we went down into the cellar of the palace; thence, by a spiral, inclined plane, we went down, down, until, by a door formed of one huge flag, and fitted to its place with remarkable exactness, we entered a small, oval room, perhaps ten feet in diameter, and hewn out of the solid rock. The door was shut behind us, and we were buried alive under the mountain! A ray of light came from above, and we could look up as through a narrow chimney; a stone was removed beneath our feet, and we could look down perhaps two or three hundred feet, and could see a little glimmer of light upon a dashing current of water, whose murmurings came up to us from beneath. And all around the room were seats cut out of the rock. And what was the object and history of this awful room?

Its history, as given us by our guide, and within its walls, is briefly as follows: In the days of feudal clemency and inquisitorial piety, those suspected of political or religious heresy were suddenly seized and confined in some of the adjacent cells. The little room above described was the room of judgment, and the judges were let down by machinery through the opening above. The accused were then introduced, and that heavy stone door was shut! And there, shut out from every eye save that of God and their judges, they were tried and condemned. If not guilty, the accused were hated or feared, which made condemnation even more certain than guilt. When condemned, they were commanded to kiss an image of the Virgin in the apartment; in the movement they touched springs, which caused her to embrace them, and in the embrace to pierce them through and through with daggers. Then a trap was sprung beneath their feet, which let their bodies fall upon a wheel armed with knives, which was kept in constant revolution by a stream of water; by those knives they were cut in pieces, and the mutilated fragments fell into the stream below!

And there we were, receiving this awful narrative in the very apartment where these atrocities were committed in the name of justice and religion, with the tunnel above us through which the holy inquisitors descended, and with the tunnel beneath us through which the bodies of their victims were let down for mutilation, so as to be beyond the reach of recognizance! For a moment our blood ran cold, and we were filled with horror! Oh! if those stone seats, and those walls of solid rock could speak—if the injunction of perpetual secrecy were removed by Him who upheaved the mountain, what awful narratives they would give of the scenes of treachery, hatred, and blood there perpetrated in the name of God and religion! What wailings were there uttered under the tortures enjoined by priests!

The stone door swung open, and we groped our way through a labyrinth of chambers and passages, dark as midnight, into the open air. We all breathed easier, and a feeling of fear gave way to one of security. We were soon after on the railway for Frankfort-on-the-Maine, deeply impressed with the beauty and wickedness of Baden-Baden, and thankful that its days of feudal and papal tyranny were at an end.

CHAPTER XXXVI.

To Frankfort from Baden-Baden.—Hôtel Russie.—The City.—Cathedral.—Jews' Quarters.—Rothschilds.—Their History, and its Lessons.—To Cassel.—Down the Rhine.—Ruins, and their History.—The Rhine and Hudson compared.—Cologne.—The Dom.—Mary and Bambino again.—The Three Kings.—The Bargain declined.—An Inference.—St. Ursula.—Bridge of Boats.

Railway sketches must be either second-hand or very imperfect. I will therefore say nothing about our ride from Baden through Heidelberg, famed for its charming situation, its university, its Catechism, its great services at the Reformation; nor of Darmstadt, a royal residence, whose drill-house for the soldiers was said by a wag to be larger than the duchy; nor of the many pretty places and vine-clad hills through which we passed, and which we saw on our way to Frankfort. The day was clear and the ride was pleasant. We reached the city of Goethe late in the afternoon, and took up our quarters at the Hôtel Russie. I find, as to this hotel, the following entry in my note-book: "Weary with the labors of the day, I lay down in a bed, which, to be comfortable, should be a foot longer or I a foot shorter. I will avoid this hotel the next time." It stands in an open, noble street, and has a reputation, like many other persons and things, wonderfully beyond its merits. I would warn all against it, save those who have the power of folding themselves up at night, and to whom such an operation is agreeable.

Frankfort has much to interest for a day or two. It is surrounded by a fertile and fine country. It is famous as a free city, and for its ancient love of republicanism, when that form of government was at a great discount in Europe. It early embraced the doctrines of the Reformation, and most of its people are now Lutherans. The new part of the city is very fine; the houses of the many rich bankers are really palaces. The old Cathedral is a very peculiar and unarchitectural building, and would seem to be the joint product of different architects greatly differing in taste and judgment, and neither yielding to the other. It was in this massive and ungainly building that the emperors of Germany were crowned for many years. We went to the Jews' quarters, where for many years they were shut up after a certain hour in the evening, and feared for a time that we were lost beyond hope, but finally got out of the narrow labyrinth, and got back in safety to our hotel. The sons of Abraham, wearing that mark on their visage which designates them equally under tropical suns and polar snows, were there in hundreds. It was in these narrow alleys the father of the Rothschilds laid the foundation of their great fortune. Nor would his widow desert her humble abode among old clothes and the poor of her people for the splendid palaces of her sons; preferring an abode among her own downtrodden and despised people to all the trappings and attentions which their more than regal wealth could purchase. A fitting mother for such sons. All honor upon such unwavering affection, even when fastidious and ill-directed.

The history of this wonderful family has its lessons.

Mayer Anselm was born in this city, in 1743, and died in 1812. Left an orphan at eleven years, he was educated for a teacher. Not liking this employment, he commenced business in a small way. He was subsequently employed in a banking-house in Hanover. By industry and frugality he saved some money, and returning to Frankfort, he established a banking-house of his own, which is still in existence. Before he was fifty years of age, he loaned the Danish government four millions of dollars! After the manner of his people, he called his sons around his dying bed, and his last words to them were respecting honesty, frugality, punctuality, and industry. And in twelve years these sons raised for different governments in Europe five hundred millions of dollars—proving them to be the most wealthy and extended banking firm in the world. Their great success they attribute to two causes—to adopt no project until examined and sanctioned by them all, and then unitedly to execute it; and to aim less at great profits than at entire security. Simple in their plans, reasonable in their terms, true to their contracts, and punctual to every engagement, they enjoy the entire confidence of the civilized world as bankers. Their letter of credit will carry a traveler, without question, round the globe. And their manners are as simple as their credit is extended. Are not principles involved and lessons taught by this brief narrative worthy the attention of all men of business? Is not honesty the best policy?

Rising early in the morning from that very short bed in that Hôtel Russie, and regaining as I could my usual dimensions, we were away for Cassel, opposite

Mayence, on the Rhine. The boat was in readiness, and soon we were steaming it at a rapid rate for Cologne. From Mayence to Bonn the scenery of the river is very fine, and is constantly changing. Ruins dating back to the Middle Ages crown every hill. As the river was the great channel of communication between the countries extending from the Alps to the North Sea, there were land pirates who erected toll-gates upon its waters, and who plundered all who would not acknowledge their authority and pay the required toll. The castles, whose ruins are every where visible, were built by these robbers. When their insolence and robberies were beyond endurance, the trading towns formed a league, raised a sufficient force and routed these robbers, and demolished their castles. Such is the brief history of those ruins, in which alone the Rhine can claim any superiority to the Hudson. If old dilapidating walls crowned all the mountains and beetling cliffs between New York and Albany—if at every bend of the river, and on every head-land, there was something to suggest legends of robbers, stories of battles fought and won, and associations running back a thousand years—in every point in which they could be compared the North River would be superior to the Rhine. People forget to what a degree their wonder and exclamations are the effects of association. Bating associations, the Rhine nowhere surpasses in wild grandeur the Highlands about West Point; nor, after you get out of sight of the Alps, has it any view to be compared to the Catskill Mountains. A few hours in a rapid boat down a rapid current brought us to our point of destination, Cologne, where, in the Hôtel Hollande, we found very pleasant accommodations, the windows overlooking the river and the country beyond.

This city, famous in all the earth for its "*eau de Cologne*," is pleasantly located, and very strongly fortified. It is of ancient date, has a varied history, and nothing but its Dom to attract the least notice. Less than ten of its eighty thousand inhabitants are Protestants; and hence, as we might expect, the churches abound in miracle-working relics. We issued out to see the Dom, as the Cathedral is called, and soon learned its direction by the old crane which yet surmounts the not half-finished tower. As far as it goes, it is the richest specimen extant of the old German architecture. Although six centuries have passed away since its foundations were laid, it is not yet one half completed; and while the stones in some part of it are new, and recently carved and laid, in other portions of it even the stones are crumbling away. In this it is a type of the Papal Church to which it belongs.

On a warm pleasant day, we wandered around its cold, vacant, but spacious interior. Nothing impresses but its vastness and the finely stained windows. We saw there a case containing Mary and Bambino, and other precious relics. The case is hung over with legs and arms, heads and hearts, made of some kind of composition, as votive offerings for cures performed by the image and the relics! And before that box there were three persons praying most earnestly; they were an old man, and a woman that would not be injured by a good washing, and a girl with sore eyes; while some women were scrubbing the stone floor and screaming at the top of their voices, and some dirty boys were playing hide-and-go-seek among the pillars.

Behind the high altar, to which none are admitted without "a compensation," there is a box which contains the relics of the Three Kings, or wise men, that worshiped the Savior. A shaven-pated man carried the keys, and he drives a hard bargain for the good of the Church. He offered to admit us to a sight of the sacred relics for six francs a head. But as there were several of us, we strove to lump a bargain with him; but he declined, thinking we would pay the sum required. But as he was stiff, we declined, obviously to his mortification, to go in at any price. Finding that neither our superstition nor our curiosity were as intense as he suspected, he proposed terms; but we declined, telling him we believed the whole a hoax at any rate. This gave the jolly man not the least offense, as he believed the same as firmly as we did. Popery is the same unchanging nonsense every where. We asked the jolly beadle what they did with the money collected from travelers and others by these relics: "We use it for the finishing of the Dom," was his reply. Judging from the dilapidation and leanness of the house, and the dress and sleek fatness of the priests, we inferred that some of it, at least, took a different direction; nor would any one say, that saw their stall-fed reverences tripping in and out, that this was a violent inference.

Here also is the church of St. Ursula, a female saint, who, with eleven thousand virgins, sailed from Britain to convert or populate Armorica. They were driven by storm up the Rhine to Cologne, where they were murdered by the barbarians, because of their unyielding virtue. And this church is hung round with their bones! Think of eleven thousand skeletons hung round one church! Where did Ursula get boats enough for such a fleet of girls? Why, in a terrific storm, did they not land before reaching Cologne? How often must these bones have been renewed from the 5th to the 19th century? And even the wonderful legend-monger, Butler, tells us that there is a doubt whether the virgins of Ursula were eleven or eleven thousand. But the eleven thousand, because the most absurd, has the benefit of the doubt. My appetite for relics was so gorged that I declined a visit to this horrid sepulchre.

By a bridge of boats Cologne is connected with a small town on the opposite bank of the Rhine. In the cool of the evening, that bridge was crowded with persons promenading back and forth, fanned by the cool breeze from the water. There we saw some of the high, and much of the low life of the city of St. Ursula. Cologne is a Papal city, and abounds with relics, priests, and beggars; and, although cleaner than we expected to find it, there are spots where the water of the Farinas', for which it is so famed, would not be unacceptable.

CHAPTER XXXVII.

From Cologne to Brussels.—Aix-la-Chapelle: its History and holy Relics.—Brussels.—The Parc.—Sabbath in Brussels.—St. Gudule. —Preaching in Flemish.—A sudden Stop.—Anecdote of Dr. Nesbit.—High Mass.—Lifting the Pay.—Tour of Observation.—Scenes in the Parc and Streets.—The Manikin: his curious History.—The miraculous Wafers.

WE took an early car from Cologne. We passed through dirty streets and strong fortifications to the railway without the walls. Although our baggage was very light, they charged nearly as much for it as for our passage. The country to Brussels is level, and highly cultivated, with quite a rapid succession of large towns; the most important of which are Duren, Aix-la-Chapelle, Verviers, Liege, Tirlemont, and Malines. Of these the most historic is Aix-la-Chapelle. Here Charlemagne was born—this was his favorite city, and here is his tomb. It is pleasantly situated in a cup surrounded by hills, on which there are many beautiful residences. It was built by the Romans, pillaged by the Huns, rebuilt by Charlemagne, and here the emperors of Germany were crowned, until the ceremony was removed to Frankfort in the fourteenth century. It is almost entirely a Papal city, and is of course rich in relics. In the Cathedral is the tomb of Charlemagne, and some antiques of priceless value. Among these are the swaddling-clothes of the Savior and his winding-sheet, the robe of the Virgin Mary, the shroud of

John the Baptist, some of the manna which fell in the wilderness, the girdle of Christ, the linen and some of the hair of the Virgin, and a fragment of the true cross. Some of these were only exposed to royal visitors; but now they are exhibited every seven years to the adoration of the faithful of every grade, when pilgrims resort here from all lands to see them, and to receive healing from their sight and touch!! Others of them are exhibited even to the gaze of heretics "for a compensation;" and if your golden key is large enough to suit the sacristan, you may have a peep even at the swaddling-clothes! In this way large revenues are yearly obtained from Protestants desirous to see curiosities, and who are often laughed at by roguish sacristans for their credulity. The object of all these base impositions is to raise a revenue. The other towns are more or less noted for the extent and perfection of their manufactures, especially those of Verviers, Liege, and Malines, famous for its Mechlin laces and shovel hats for priests. Late in the afternoon we reached Brussels, the capital of Belgium, and soon found ourselves very pleasantly accommodated in the Hôtel de France, which looks out upon the beautiful Parc.

Brussels is a pleasant, airy, and attractive city, with many fine streets and parks, and wearing a general aspect which forcibly recalls your recollections of Paris. Indeed, it has been called "petit Paris." And nowhere are you so forcibly reminded of the city on the Seine as in and around "the Parc," bounded by the Rue Royale and Rue Ducale, and having the palace at one end and the representative chamber on the other. The trees are old and magnificent, shading all the walks;

and beneath the trees and along all the walks are pieces of statuary more or less elegant, and in varying states of preservation, as in the gardens of the Tuileries and the Place de Concorde. The city was once strongly fortified, but the walls are demolished, and the place they once occupied is laid out so as to form a beautiful drive around the entire city. Some of the public buildings are very fine, but they should be seen before making a continental tour, instead of at the close of it, as in our case.

We spent a Sabbath in Brussels, the last we spent in a Papal country, and among a people of a strange tongue. As there was no Protestant service in our own tongue, we went to the Cathedral of St. Gudule in the morning to see the home dress of Popery in one of its strong-holds. This is a fine specimen of Gothic architecture, and has all the elements of a Cathedral—no seats—many chairs—painted windows—a spacious interior—many altars and confession-boxes, and a profusion of gilding. The painted windows are very fine. Its internal appearance is very meagre in comparison with the churches of Rome. In Rome every thing yields to the interior. A building which externally has no attraction, like that of Ara Cœli, is internally gorgeous, and rich in painting and statuary; but out of Italy it would seem as if architecture was the great idea, and to which every thing is made to yield. Art rules south—architecture north of the Alps.

We went to St. Gudule before the hour for high mass, which was that day performed. A priest was preaching in the Flemish to quite an audience of people, and the waiters were arranging the chairs and moving in every direction making arrangements for the high ceremony. People were walking about and chatting with one another. A more inattentive audience could not be desired; and were I the preacher, I could not endure the confusion. Just as the clock struck ten, a beadle walked up the pulpit-stairs, the preacher closed his discourse in an instant, crossed himself and walked down and away, the beadle leading the van. The instance forcibly recalled another anecdote of Dr. Nesbit. He was in the habit of preaching sermons in the good long metre of Scotland. A committee waited on him, and kindly hinted that short metre would be more acceptable to many of the people. On inquiry, he learned that a sermon an hour long would suit them all; he assented to the shortening. On the next Sabbath, just as the hour was drawing to its close, he became exceedingly animated, interesting, eloquent, and impressive. In the midst of a highly-wrought passage, the hour ended; and, without waiting to conclude the sentence, he closed his Bible, paused for a moment, and said, "Brethren, your hour is out; let us pray."

On the retiring of the preacher, the mass commenced, and the people turned from the pulpit to the altar. We never saw priests more richly robed. The vestments at St. Gudule far surpassed those worn in the Sistine or in St. Peter's. Nor did we ever see in a Popish church a more numerous or respectable congregation. But, with slight variations, it was the same ridiculous farce of the mass over again; and in the midst of the high ceremony, an interstice was left for "lifting the pay" from every man, woman, and child that sat on a chair. And it seemed to us most singular to see the collectors paying back the change to those who gave silver. For at least fifteen or twenty minutes the whole house was turned into an exchange, in every part of which was heard the jingling of coppers. And we thought of the money-changers in the Temple.

In the afternoon we went out on a tour of moral inspection. In the midst of "the Parc" rises a mound, and on that mound rises a building in the form of a canopy, in which was a very large band of musicians. Around this mound is a wide circular walk finely shaded with magnificent trees, and filled on both sides with chairs. The band on each fair Sabbath day commences playing at one o'clock, and continues to three; and during the intervening time, the entire Parc is filled with the élite, the fashion, the gay attire of Brussels. The band plays, and the people—men, women, and children—all march. We never beheld such luxury of dress as was there worn by the ladies.

The sight would have been gorgeous and fascinating were it not for its flagrant violation of the Sabbath. From the Parc we went out among some of the principal streets; the shops were all open, and most gayly decorated, and were filled with purchasers, among whom we recognized many priests. We went to the most fashionable church in the city to evening mass, in which we counted three men and about two hundred women and children. After dusk we took another stroll through the city. The shops were crowded—porter-houses and cafés were all open, and crowded with men and women! the women often more numerous than the men! Such was the state of things on this beautiful Sabbath, in the beautiful little city of

Brussels. Another item in proof of the fact that Popery knows no Sabbath. And as I retired to rest, I uttered my sincere thanksgiving to God that this was the last Sabbath I expected to spend amid the institutions of Popery, and among people of a strange tongue.

The city is ornamented and supplied with seven fountains, among which are Les Fontaines des Fleuves and the Manikin. This latter is the bronze figure of an urchin-boy about two feet high, who discharges a stream of water in a natural way. The people of the city regard the questionable figure with great veneration, as the palladium of their rights and liberties. The fate of the city is superstitiously regarded as identified with the fate of this not very modest boy of bronze. When stolen, as has been frequently the case, his loss was regarded as a public calamity; and his restoration has been always commemorated with fêtes. Princes have courted popularity with the people by presenting him with court dresses, and military honors and orders. The Elector of Bavaria gave him a splendid wardrobe and a valet de chambre. Louis XV. made him a knight, and presented him with a suit of uniform. This little gentleman is dressed up on certain days, when the city turns out to do him honor. He possesses a positive revenue, which is regularly paid to him; but how he spends it we could not learn. It was suggested that some bishop or monk was his treasurer. As the suggestion is not unreasonable, we may readily conjecture what becomes of the revenue of "Sir Manikin." He has become rather republican in his notions, and, since 1830, wears the uniform of the "Garde Civique," in preference to those of his royal donors. And as we gazed upon the little urchin filling the kettles and vessels of men and women who came to him for water, we were amazed at the stupid superstition of the people, and at the wicked craft of kings and princes who could seek to ingratiate themselves with the people by heaping honors upon such a bawble! Had the priests done this it would be all in their line. But they are not without their fraudulent relics in Brussels; they have in the Cathedral the three miraculously consecrated wafers, said to have been stolen by the Jews in the fourteenth century, and to have been discovered by their miraculous spouting of blood when pierced with a spear by an unbeliever! These are shown "for a compensation," and are annually exhibited with great pomp for the veneration of the faithful! O priests, priests, where are your blushes?

CHAPTER XXXVIII.

To Waterloo.—The Village.—The Field.—Just the Place for the Battle.—The dreadful Spot.—Feelings excited there.—Conjectures.—Justice to Bonaparte.—What has England gained?—Through Flanders to Ostend.—The Hulk.—Rapid Flight.

We took an early breakfast in Brussels, and started for Waterloo, at the distance of ten or twelve miles. Without being as bad as many travelers would represent it, the road and ride through the forest of Soignies is not very interesting. We went on with rapid pace, and at about nine o'clock we were in Waterloo, a most miserable-looking village. As we approached it we were beset by many learned in the localities of the place, and most kindly offering their services as guides. We employed a resident of the place, who most kindly introduced us to his wife and daughter, who had relics collected from the battle-field to sell. We proceed to the scene of carnage, and from the position which Wellington occupied, and where he uttered the command, "Up, and be at them!" we took our first, deliberate, silent view of the field of blood. Nor is there a solitary thing to arrest your attention in the field itself. If that artificial pile of clay called "La Montagne du Lion," surmounted by the Belgian lion with his paw upon a globe, to represent little Belgium as governing this big world, were scattered, as it ought to be, over the plain from which it was collected—if the monuments here and there erected to commemorate the military virtues of men that were there made to bite the dust, were removed—if the great contest which there decided the peace of Europe could be forgotten, it would be difficult to select a more uninteresting dead-level view than that which opens up before you. The plain extends, rich in cultivation, but level as the sea, as far as the eye can reach on three sides, and the forest of Soignies lies on the other. And yet one can readily conceive that it was just the place to fight such a great battle. There are no fences or ditches to arrest the movements of men, artillery, or cavalry. There are no hiding-places for cowards. An elevation of less than one hundred feet would enable a commander to review the army of Xerxes; and, until I looked over the wide, level plain, I had no conception of a position where two armies, so vast in number, could fight, retreat, deploy—where cavalry could rush to the aid of infantry—where flying artillery could appear and fire, and, before the smoke of the cannon had risen from the earth, be out of the reach of the shot of the enemy. It is just the place for such a fierce and fearful conflict.

About a mile beyond the insignificant village or hamlet of Waterloo, you reach an eminence which rises on the vast plain like a wave on the sea. You pass down into what may be regarded as the furrow of the wave, and ascend another wave at a short distance. Along the ridge of the first wave the British forces, under Wellington, were drawn up; on the ridge of the other, the French, under Napoleon. And the furrow between them was the scene of awful carnage. On the 18th of June, 1815, one hundred and fifty thousand men lined these ridges, nearly equally divided by the vale between them. The battle commenced about noon, and lasted until night. And there I was standing on the very spot where Wellington exclaimed, when the battle was obviously against him, "O that Blucher or night might come!" and a little further on is the spot where, inspirited by the appearance of the Prussians, he gave the brief order to a concealed prostrate company, "Up, and at them!" as the "Old Guard" was crossing the valley under the brave Ney. We walked over the valley, on that fearful day crowded with the heroic dead, and flowing with blood, and in a few minutes we were on the spot where Napoleon stood when he ordered his Imperial Guard, which had never been conquered, and which was the terror of Europe, to the deadly breach under Ney, saying, "This, gentlemen, is the road to Brussels!" Never was an attack more valorously made; never was an attack more firmly met or more fearfully repulsed. Under the awful and repeated fire of the British, the Guard recoiled, soon was thrown into confusion, and the field of Waterloo was lost to Napoleon!

It was on the last day of June we wandered over this field of blood. And the two eminences—where stood the two greatest generals of modern days—were waving with yellow wheat, and the valley that divides them was bearing rich grass ready for the scythe of the mower. And every thing seemed as quiet as if the roaring of canon was never there heard, and as innocent as if the cruel war had never there perpetrated the bloodiest acts known in the annals of the world. And standing by the tomb of one of the heroic dead, and in view of the unsightly mountain, two hundred feet high, beneath which the bones of friends and foes lie peaceful in death, I felt intensely moved in view of the awful carnage of that battle—of the destinies it decided—of the wailing and lamentation which it spread through Europe, whose every country and island made some contribution to its piles of dead—and of the subsequent fate of the chief actors in the bloody tragedy. There the star of Napoleon set to rise no more; Napoleon, the greatest military genius of a hundred ages, and of the most capacious and comprehensive intellect. And while walking over the ground where the last tragic scene of his great military life was enacted, every sympathy of my heart went out toward the fallen chieftain, whose history is yet to be truly written, and whose motives and character will yet be placed in their true light.

If victory had followed the great hero to Waterloo, as to Jena, Austerlitz, Marengo, and Lodi, we may not be able to conjecture what results would have followed, but we may state what would not have followed. The old Bourbon dynasty, restored by the Holy Alliance, would not have again cursed France. Bloody Austria would never have reached her present bad preeminence in the politics of Europe. Russia would not sit as now upon her icy throne, hurling defiance at all national aspirations after freedom, and coolly contemplating the speediest and easiest way of converting into Cossacks all the people and nations from the North Cape to the Dardanelles, and from the Volga at least to the Rhine, if not to the English Channel. Poland would not have been blotted from the map of the world. The tragedy of Hungary would not have been enacted. The fearful murders perpetrated in the name of justice, and for the purpose of maintaining the claims of legitimacy, which have stained every nation of Continental Europe, would not have occurred. The Two Sicilies, as now, would not be groaning under burdens beyond human endurance. And Popery, as now, would not be arrogantly asserting its exploded claims, and making of even its mutilated and paralyzed form an argument for the admission of those claims! It was not with the progress of the race, but with the permanency of despotic institutions, religious and civil, that Bonaparte warred. He was ambitious, but it was to carry his objects. And if that ambition took the form of selfishness and of self-aggrandizement, it was the better to carry his objects. If he could do his work as well by being consul or president as by being emperor, he would have preferred it. And we have faith to believe that his conduct, which lay in the direction of selfishness, was not of choice, but of necessity. If he were as bad a man as British historians of the Tory school would represent him, it is impossible that he could be, as he now is, enshrined in the heart of hearts of the French nation. It is not in human nature to make a demi-god of the devil.

And what has England gained, save a monstrous national debt, by the overthrow of Napoleon? She mainly contributed to that end: without her men and means, the French would have swept all the other allies from the field of Waterloo by the first fire of her cannon. And what has she gained in Europe by her service? Absolutely nothing that she would not now have if she had cultivated friendly relations with the empire and its emperor, while Europe besides would be in all respects the gainer. The defeat of Napoleon at Waterloo was the triumph of despotism over freedom—of divine right over the rights of the people; and well and nobly did Robert Hall exclaim, when he heard of the victory of Wellington at Waterloo, "*That battle and its results seem to me to have put back the clock of the world six degrees.*" And England may yet reap the rewards of her evil doing in her constant and successful opposition to the plans and projects of Napoleon Bonaparte.

We paid our guide; and, although we gave him the wages of a whole day for a few hours, he besought us for "charity." We returned to Brussels, and late in the afternoon took the cars for Ostend. Although our road lay through Flanders, and the cities of Ghent and Bruges, such was the rapidity of our travel that we could see but little. Nor did we stop at Ostend long enough to have any experience of its odors, which are said to be not quite agreeable. We hastened on board "The English and Belgian Royal Mail Steamer," of which we might say all that we said, and more, of the boat that conveyed us from Dover to Calais. From ten o'clock in the evening to five o'clock in the morning, seven mortal hours, we spent in the awful hulk. The fare was high, and there was no place for repose save the floor and benches. The sea was calm; but the thing called a cabin was decidedly hot. We could not secure even a drink of cold water. And yet, before we reached Dover, two officials of her majesty came upon us with a demand for half a dollar each for attendance!

We were on the field of Waterloo at twelve o'clock on Monday; were in Brussels at five; at Ostend at ten; in Dover at five in the morning of Tuesday; and at eight we were at breakfast in the very heart of the city of London. This seemed more like annihilating distance than any thing we had yet experienced. And we rendered our devout thanks to God that we were again in a land of civil and religious liberty, and among a people whose language was our own.

CHAPTER XXXIX.

Fleetwood.—Bathing Establishment.—State-room Companion.—Landing in Ireland.—Introduction to the Assembly.—Dr. Cook.—Dr. Edgar.—Dr. Stewart.—Dr. Dobbin.—Dr. Carlisle.—Dr. Dill.—Dr. Goudy.—An excited Scene.—Great Speech of Dr. Cook.—Two Bodies compared.—The Irish Way.—A more excellent Way.

Learning, on reaching London, that the General Assembly of the Presbyterian Church of Ireland had commenced its annual sessions at Belfast, I hastened thither to meet it. Taking the Express train, we were in a few hours at Fleetwood, on the Irish Sea. This is a new town, and is rising rapidly as a bathing and watering place. There is here the largest, neatest, and most convenient bathing establishment I ever saw. At high tide, the salt water runs into a reservoir; thence it is thrown up by steam power into an immense basin; and thence it is conducted by pipes to all the apartments, which seemed endless. The engine which pumps, also heats water for tepid baths; so that you can swim, plunge, bathe, or take the shower, in cold or warm water, at any range of the thermometer, at a minute's notice, and for sixpence! It seemed a perfect establishment.

"This is our best state-room, and you can have the upper berth in it," said the steward to me, as I went on board the steamer for Ireland. Anxious to know who would occupy the lower shelf, I asked him who would be my room-mate. "Dr. Cook, a minister in

Belfast," was his reply; the man of all others in Ireland I wished most to see. Having learned who he was, I eyed him with all the powers of my scrutiny. We met in the state-room. We each commenced gradual approaches—each knew the name of the other, and soon we ventured on a mutual introduction. Having tickled each other a little after the Irish fashion, we went to our shelves, and talked until the claims of sleep became irresistible. The night was fine, but the sea was unquiet. Amid a glowing sun and a refreshing air, we entered the bay of Belfast, and soon reached the quays of the city. And as I went forth from the deck of the steamer my emotions became unutterable, and I could not help exclaiming with joy,

"My foot it treads my native soil;
I breathe my native air."

O how changed in years, in mind, in heart, in all the circumstances of my being, from what I was when, upward of thirty years previous, youthful, unknown, and friendless, I went forth from that land to seek my fortune in the new world of the West! Soon I was in my room at the "Imperial," where, I trust, I returned my thanksgivings to God for his varied mercies and goodness during the many years intervening between my departure and my return. And never did the sweet hymn of Addison possess to me the meaning and the unction which it did on that occasion:

"When all thy mercies, O my God,
My rising soul surveys,
Transported with the view, I'm lost
In wonder, love, and praise!"

As soon as my arrival was known, Dr. Dill and Mr.

Simpson, well known in America and highly esteemed, waited on me and conducted me to the Assembly, and introduced me to many of its leading members. Nothing could be more cordial than their hearty welcome. On the arrival of Dr. W. S. Brackenridge, we were both, on the motion of Dr. Dill, seconded by Dr. Edgar, unanimously invited to sit in the Assembly, and to take part in its deliberations. No attention that Christian courtesy could suggest was withheld from us.

The Irish General Assembly, unlike that of Scotland and of the United States, is not a representative body from Presbyteries; it is rather constituted as are our synods. Every Presbyterian minister in the kingdom, connected with any of its Presbyteries, is entitled to a seat, and every Church is entitled to its delegate. Considering the number of ministers and churches, this makes a large body of the Assembly; far too large for calm, judicious deliberation. All that we saw deeply impressed us with this conviction. The Assembly seemed to us like a great Presbyterian mass-meeting, where addresses are made for popular effect. With one tenth the number of members, it would have done as wisely, and more calmly and rapidly.

The great men of the Church were there, and under sufficient excitement to bring out all their peculiar force and talent. Dr. Cook was there, of middle stature, firmly built, and, although advanced in life, with natural energies unabated. His face is long, his nose Roman, his hair and eyes gray, his lips thin and compressed, and his forehead expanded. He was obviously the man of the House, in debate. The conflict as to the founding of a college under the will of Mrs. Magee, between her trustees and the Assembly, excited all his energies. His invectives are terrible; his acting very fine; his wit keen; his sarcasm withering. He sometimes fell upon his opponents like a tornado. Dr. John Edgar was there, rough in appearance, not handsome in form or feature, rather inclining to a semicircle when he walks or sits, blunt in conversation, honest and downright in his opinions and expression of them, intelligent, influential in debate, truly and subjectively pious, with a heart as warm as ever beat in an Irishman's body, and a nature all tending to the poetic and philanthropic. "Where," said I, as I entered the Assembly, "is Dr. Edgar?" "There he is yonder," said my friend, "with his head between his knees." No man in Ireland is more esteemed or useful. And Dr. Stewart was there—since deceased—tall, slender, calm, logical, in many respects the most able man in the house, and obviously a leader. His social qualities were of the highest order. Dr. Dobbin was there, fair in complexion, rotund in form, of fine countenance, and always wearing glasses. He often spoke, and ably. Dr. Carlisle was there, slender in person, tall, with a fine head, thin gray hair, tender eyes, and a most benevolent expression. He was very retiring. I did not hear him speak once. His name is revered in Ireland for his great piety and his missionary labors. Dr. Duff paid him a most glowing tribute as an apostolical missionary in one of his Belfast orations. Dr. Dill was there, of strong muscular development, which was sometimes needed in his conflicts with the priests; calm, able in debate, in labors abundant, and esteemed by all for his piety and for his services in the Irish mission field. Mr. Dill, of Dublin, was there; short, but strongly framed; able in debate; and as one of the trustees of Mrs. Magee, the leader of the side of the house which went with the trustees for the location of the college in Derry. Dr. Kirkpatrick was there; small in person, of sandy complexion, always wearing glasses, speaking rarely, but beloved for his amiable, unobtrusive piety. And others were there, truly Irish in appearance, accent, and excitability, and the most violent men I ever saw in a deliberative body, save and always in the French Chamber of Deputies. One of these was the Rev. Dr. Goudy, whose acquaintance I had not the pleasure of making. His excitement rose at times almost to frenzy. When in his highest mood, he seemed like an incarnation of passion.

Although warned on all hands not to judge of the Assembly generally by what I had seen during my visit, I will describe a scene which I witnessed in the church of Dr. Cook.

The Assembly met at eleven o'clock in the morning, and adjourned at five for dinner; it met again at seven, and often sat until two next morning. Dining in company with several eminent clergymen, we did not get back to the Assembly until about eight o'clock. The church was densely thronged; we entered from the rear, and found the house in a perfect uproar. The moderator was standing and calling to order; fifty persons were striving to speak: one would cry out, "Vote;" another, "No, no;" another, "The roll." One would rise, shouting "I rise to a point of order;" another would ask for "the civil power;" another would shout, "Turn them out!" There were cheers and hisses from the crowded galleries; these were echoed from the floor;

and now and then, from floor to roof, nothing was heard but confused noises, which the moderator could no more quell than a child could tame a tempest. Dr. Cook rose in the middle aisle, and got the admission of the chair that he had the floor. But how to maintain it and go on was the question! And there for nearly two hours he battled, with remarkable skill and dexterity, the storm, repelling assaults from all sides, and administering some withering rebukes to some that would interrupt him. His perseverance succeeded; he maintained the floor; the intense excitement subsided, and he delivered the great speech of the Assembly, and in the best style of his best days. For upward of two hours the vast crowd hung upon his lips; at one moment, such was the anxiety to catch his lower tones, you could hear your heart beat; and at another, some of his keen and terrible sarcasms would bring the vast audience to their feet in boisterous applause. The question was taken long after midnight, and the doctor carried the vote by a large majority. His deliverance on that evening was said to be equal to any of his great efforts, when in the vigor of his manhood he contended with Arianism in the synod of Ulster.

The two most excited deliberative bodies I ever saw were the French National and the Irish General Assembly. Which was the most excited it would be difficult to determine. And yet it was pleasant to see, on the day after that stormy debate, the fiercest opponents walking arm in arm in the streets of Belfast, and treating each other with all good feeling on the floor of the House. The Irish have certainly a way of doing things peculiar to themselves; and because in a real row every body pours out their entire feelings, there is no remaining sediment; and when their feelings cool, they meet as friends. They fight it out, and then all is over. And all this is far preferable to hiding jealous, envious, rancorous feeling in our hearts, which nothing can charm or allay:

> "Which will not list to wisdom's lore,
>   Nor music's voice can lure it;
> But there it stings for evermore
>   The heart that must endure it."

On the whole, I go for the Irish way of settling difficulties. "If any man have a quarrel against any," fight it out fairly, and then forbear, and forgive one another. I have no patience with the piety which restrains hard words, and which nourishes hard feelings forever. Yet the more excellent way is to indulge only right feelings, and to utter only soft words, which turn away wrath.

CHAPTER XL.

Visit to Connaught.—Sligo.—Emigrants.—Often remove for the Worse.—Camline.—Famine Scenes.—A young Hero.—The Dead Ass and Family.—Industrial Schools.—Several visited.—Priestly Outrages.—Visit at Home.—Great Changes.—Dublin.—Mr. King.—Dr. Urwick.—An Incident.—A brighter Day coming.

As on some future occasion I may treat of Ireland and the Irish in a separate volume, I must dismiss for the present all accounts of my very pleasant visit to that island with a few brief sketches.

In company with Dr. Edgar, I made a flying visit to Connaught, to see for myself what has been always regarded as the most dark and uncivilized portion of the country. We passed through Lisburn, Moira, Lurgan, Armagh, Monaghan, to Enniskillen, and thence to Sligo, where we first saw the opening of Connaught wretchedness. It was a market-day in Sligo, and we went all over the town. The people were poorly clad, generally peaceable in their demeanor, and the matters and things for sale were of the most primitive character. As we approached this little sea-port, we passed a few small companies of persons which seemed to be deeply affected; and on inquiry we learned that they were friends accompanying their friends to the ship which was to convey them to America. Many, many emigrants there are who sever the endearing ties of kindred and home, and leave their scanty, yet comfortable competence, and go out from influences that would bind them to temperance and virtue to the close of life, to become hewers of wood and drawers of water in America, and to descend through the grog-shop to intemperance, crime, and infamy, and to sink into a premature grave, over which a tear is never shed.

From Sligo we proceeded to Boyle, where we were met by a private carriage, which conveyed us to Camline, the residence of a noble specimen of an Irish lady, and the young widow of a man belonging to the old Irish gentry. And now I was in the famine district of Ireland, and under the roof of a lady who, with a sister, remained to minister to the living and the dying, when all others fled as from the breath of the pestilence. They described to me scenes of which they were the witnesses, which rendered me nervous and wakeful through the night. A poor mother died of famine; the father went to a town for meal, and got none; returning home, he leaned against a turf-rick in the bog and died, leaving three orphan children. The children were taken with the famine fever; one, in her delirium, ran to the bog, fell into a hole, and was drowned. Missed by her sick brother, he rose and went in search of her. He drew her body from the hole, and, unable to carry it, drew it to the house; and when my informant saw it, the body was laid out by the hands of that sick brother upon the cabin door, which was taken from its hinges for that purpose. That boy alone survived of the family. Could I have found him, I would have brought him to America. He was a hero in his way.

They told of another family that killed their ass for

food, and put away its meat in a barrel. The family died, and their bodies and the meat of the ass were found putrefying together! So many died, and so many were sick and unable to bury them, that many were interred in the ruins of their cabins, which were pulled down upon their lifeless occupants! And the ruins of desolate villages, once populous, but now utterly deserted, we daily met in our rambles in Connaught.

Through the very efficient and intelligent agency of Dr. Edgar, much is doing in Connaught through industrial schools, in which the children are taught "to learn and to earn." I visited several of these at Camline, Clogher, Newpark, Dromore West, Ballina, Owenmore, and others. They are mostly under the care of lady patronesses, and some of them are superintended by missionaries of the General Assembly. In the way of the instruction of the children in morals and religion, and into habits of industry, they are doing an incalculable amount of good. I have seen one hundred children in some of these schools, who, while they were securing a good education, earned more by their needles in working muslin than could their fathers by their daily labor. I frequently examined them as to their knowledge of the great principles of religion, and of the plan of salvation; and, although the children of Popish parents, they would compare most favorably with any children of a similar age that I have ever met in our best-regulated and best-instructed Sunday-schools. Of course, the priests bitterly oppose them, and hate them with an intense hatred. They not unfrequently flog the children for going, and the parents for permitting them to go! The priests have made Ireland a godless,

Christless land, and thus they have debased and cursed it. And the only cure for Ireland is that which these schools is applying, to instruct and to evangelize the people. When the knowledge of the Bible and of Jesus Christ supplants the wretched idolatry of Popery, the days of Ireland's mourning are ended.

I made, of course, a visit to the home of my childhood, the remembrances of which were fast passing away from my mind. And the difference between my boyish recollections and things as I found them surprised me. The river of my boyhood was a small streamlet over which I could step; the mountain was a little hillock; the lake was a pond over which an Indian could shoot his arrow; the road, two miles long, became remarkably shortened; and the town, which was quite large, and with fine buildings, although not diminished, was only a small village, and with very indifferent houses. There were three spots which I well remember: the place where the school-house stood, where I first learned the alphabet, but the house and my old teacher were gone; the spring, from which I drew many a cooling draught; and the place in the grave-yard where my father was buried before I was six years of age, and to which my mother used to take me often by the hand. Although more than forty years had passed away since I entered the walls of that parish cemetery, I went directly to that hallowed grave.

O the changes which a few years make in any locality to those returning on a visit! On reaching my childish home, that was gone, and another house had taken its place. An older brother, a joyous youth when we parted, now met me almost an old man. His wife and children were entire strangers. Not one that I left in midlife remained. Not a trace existed of entire families. An old lady said she remembered me "a fine bright chap going to school;" and a few persons, a little older or younger than myself, said they would know me any where, which was very questionable. This was all the remembrance I could eke out. I stood in the presence of a younger brother some minutes without his suspecting who I was; and when introduced, he was overwhelmed with surprise. The old neighbors were all gone, and the houses of many of them torn down. I called to see a relative that I remembered as a youthful, blooming bride when a boy at school, and I found her old, and haggard, and sickly, and, in the vain effort to keep herself warm, sitting over a fire in July! And the thought flashed over me that I was advancing in years! My school-mates were all gone save one, who told me that I gave him a knife by which to remember me; but I had forgotten even his name. Nobody knew me, and I knew nobody! Whether or not it was the effect of my feelings, I became sick. I could not bear up under the emotions that were constantly rising on my mind and soul, like waves on a stormy ocean, and after a more brief visit than I intended to make, I ordered my car and was away Never had I such a feeling sense of the meaning of these words of David: "As for man, his days are as grass; as a flower of the field so he flourisheth. For the wind passeth over it and it is gone, and the place thereof shall know it no more."

I would be doing great injustice to all my feelings should I close this brief sketch of my visit to Ireland without any notice of Dublin and the dear friends there. The house of the Rev. Alexander King, the eloquent, fearless, faithful defender of Protestantism, whose eloquent deliverances in America are not soon to be forgotten by us, was my home, where I was treated as a brother. The attentions of Dr. Urwick, small in person, unimpressive in appearance, but with a heart and mind of the noblest development, were of the most paternal kind. I was deeply impressed with an incident which occurred at his table. Dr. Baird, who had just landed from America, was there. "I saw your son a short time ago in New York," said he, addressing Mrs. Urwick, who has since gone to heaven. He was the first person she saw who had seen that son in the New World. It was too much for her weak frame. She rose from the table, unable to restrain her emotions, and retired. Who but a mother knows the depths of a mother's heart? And with Dr. Kirkpatrick and the Rev. Richard Dill I was permitted to renew the acquaintance which I had the pleasure to make with them at Belfast And the favors conferred upon me by these brethren, and by other distinguished citizens of Dublin, at a public meeting in the Rotunda, and at a public breakfast at Freemason's Tavern, in Dame Street, will be ever and gratefully remembered.

A better and brighter day is dawning upon Ireland. Education is extending among the people. The power of the priest, which has only been a power for evil, is giving way. The Protestant Churches are waking up to a sense of their high missions to the people. The ministers of the Established Church begin to feel that they should do something for the salvation of the people, who have only known them as fox and hare hunters, fine livers, and tithe proctors. The lands are passing out of the hands of bankrupt proprietors into those of persons of wealth, who can improve them and relieve the tenants. The vast exodus of the Papal population to this and other lands is making way for English and Scotch farmers, who are going over in large numbers, and carrying with them Protestantism and habits of industry. And the prospect is most promising, that by the blessing of God upon these and other means which are quietly at work, Ireland will again assume the position which ages ago she held for intelligence, religion, and high civilization among the nations of the earth. When all her people are educated—when the religion of the Bible is received by them, then the jealousies of sects and of races will come to an end—priestly agitations will be known no more; and, like a tempest-tossed vessel anchoring in a quiet harbor, it will quietly rest under the smile of God.

CHAPTER XLI.

Down the Liffey.—Up the Clyde.—Glasgow.—John Henderson.—The Cathedral.—Necropolis.—M'Gavin.—Communion Service.—Tokens and Tables.—Pew Communion.—Dr. Gordon.—The Irish Mission.—Gaelic Chapel.—Dr. Candlish.—Model School.—Examination.—A Dinner-party.—Edinburgh described.

It was five o'clock in the afternoon when I bid farewell to the dear friends of Dublin, and when the steamer "Vanguard" turned her prow down the Liffey for Glasgow. And I thought of the day when, a youth, I sailed down the same waters in the "Martha," to seek a home beyond the waves of the Atlantic. And what induced me, yet a lad, thus to throw myself on the world? The hand of God was in it. I went out, not knowing whither I went; but God knew. Soon we passed Kingston and Howth; and as the shores of Ireland receded from view, and the heavings of the blue sea commenced exciting some symptoms of internal commotion, I went quietly to my shelf, leaving the "Vanguard" to make her way through the Channel without my guidance or care. I awoke in the Firth of the Clyde, in the morning. Soon we left the barren hills of Arran behind us; soon those of Bute. After stopping an hour at Greenock, we continued our course by Dumbarton Castle and town to Glasgow, where we arrived at noon.

The sail up the Clyde is pleasant, and, to a stranger, interesting. The hills are treeless, and covered only with heather. The houses on the water's edge are without any shelter. Villages are frequent, and wear an appearance of neatness. Above Greenock, the channel of the river becomes winding and narrow, and the navigation slow and difficult; and while the scenery is pleasing, every thing is on a cabinet scale. It bears scarcely a comparison with a sail up the Hudson.

Glasgow is the Manchester of Scotland, and is increasing like an American city. It has now a population of 360,000, while in 1830 it had only about 200,000. While almost exclusively a commercial city, it has several literary, and many charitable and philanthropic institutions. Its churches are numerous—many of its clergy have an American as well as a European reputation; and many of its princely merchants consecrate their wealth and influence to arrest the tide of wickedness flowing in upon it because of its mercantile and manufacturing prosperity. Among these are John Henderson, of Park, one of the co-laborers of Sir Andrew Agnew on the better sanctification of the Sabbath, and upon whom the mantle of the departed baronet seems to have fallen.

The old Cathedral and the Necropolis alone possessed any peculiar interest to me. The first is almost the only ecclesiastical building of the Middle Ages left north of the Tweed, and is venerable for its antiquity; but, interiorly, the unity of its design is entirely destroyed by its being fitted up for Protestant worship. Its crypt is said to be one of the finest in Europe, in which, our guide informed us, lie buried the remains of Irving. The Necropolis, which is the Père la Chaise of Glasgow, forms a fine background to the Cathedral, from which it is separated by a small streamlet or "burn," which babbles along its stony bed to the Clyde. On passing over this burn on "the Bridge of Sighs," you ascend up by a steep, winding path; and when you reach the summit of the grounds, the Cathedral of St. Mungo and Glasgow lie at your feet. The view from this point is extended for such a hilly country, and is very fine. There are two monuments which arrest the attention of every visitor: the first and most conspicuous is that erected to the memory of John Knox; and the other is that erected to perpetuate the memory of M'Gavin, the author of "The Protestant," and who was a banker and merchant of this city. He was a man of learning, piety, philanthropy; and although his memory is blackened in every way by papal bishops and "the *inferior* clergy," it is held in the very highest repute by the people of Glasgow. Were they not such stanch Protestants, and were it not for the fear of placing him in bad company, they would put him in the calendar. They know too much of the history of papal saints to place their noble and fearless fellow-citizen on a par with such ignorant and wicked sensualists and fanatics. The time from Glasgow to Edinburgh is less than two hours; and I reached the Athens of the North late on Saturday evening.

My first Sabbath in Scotland was a most interesting one. It was communion at Free St. Mary's, of which the venerable and beloved Dr. Henry Gray is pastor. As we entered the church, a table with plates on it, and around which stood several persons, first presented itself. All that entered placed some money on the plates. And this custom we observed every where in

Scotland where we worshiped. When the people go up to worship God, they are "careful to remember the poor." This saves from our unseemly way of taking up collections, whether with plates or with bags, which often detracts more from the solemnity of a service than the collections benefit. The pastor, wearing his gown and bands, feeble in health, thin, and tall in person, preached a sweet sermon, and with great unction, on the text, "Christ in you the hope of glory." Tables and tokens were used. The first table was served by Dr. Cunningham; and when its service was ended, nearly all that communicated retired from the house. The younger communicants retired at the close of the sermon, but returned in time to commune at the last tables. As each table has a service of its own, and often from a different clergyman, it makes of the whole ceremony a very protracted affair. And while impressed with the solemnity of the service, and with the very weighty and important exhortations made, and with the large number of youth that partook of the sacrament, we could not help the conviction that "tokens and tables," without adding any thing, greatly detracted from the unity, the solemnity, and impressiveness of the entire service, and tend greatly to the weariness of pastor and people. Pew communion, as with us, where the old and young met together without noise or changing of seats, where all remain until the service is ended, where all are invited to partake who make a credible profession of religion, placing the responsibility of partaking unworthily upon themselves, we believe to be the more excellent way. The rule which would bind us in this matter to the way of our Scotch and

Irish ancestry, is better in the breach than in the observance.

We went in the afternoon to hear Dr. Gordon in his new edifice by the new college of the Free Church. His congregation was large and attentive. The doctor is a small, lean man, past sixty years of age, with thin gray hair, high forehead, and with a general expression of countenance more amiable than intellectual. With a feeble, but yet distinct and effective voice, he preached an excellent sermon. The seat of his elders is on a range with the pulpit, and almost as high; among whom sat Dr. Duff. Dr. Cunningham is one of his elders. As a pious, judicious man, consecrated to his work, and safe in all his measures and influences, Dr. Gordon stands very high in Britain.

As Dr. Candlish was advertised to preach in the Gaelic chapel, under the shadow of the castle, in the evening, I took a long walk to hear him. Following a crowd, I pressed my way into a circular building to a position where I had a full view of what was going on. The pulpit, standing on one side near the floor, was occupied by two ministers, while seats rose one above another to the very roof; and these seats all the way up were crowded densely with a most interested auditory. The men in the pulpit were asking questions of persons on the opposite side of the house, and on the highest seats. They replied in a peculiar accent, and often asked questions in turn. Persons through the house asked questions, and often interposed. Sheridan Knowles sat near the pulpit, and addressed the people. Dr. Begg was there and spoke. Somebody said something about the Savior reducing the Ten Commandments to two, while the Papists made two of one, and thus made eleven commandments. "And sure," said a man with a droll voice and accent, throwing a broad smile over the whole auditory, "and sure, if you Protestants *can* get along with two commandments, we Roman Catholics *ought to be able* to get along with eleven." Astonished at all I saw and heard, I asked, "Is that Dr. Candlish, and is this the Gaelic chapel?" "Oh, no," said the person I addressed, "this is the service of the Irish mission; Dr. Candlish is preaching in the church opposite." The chief man in the pulpit was the Rev. Peter M'Menomy, a converted Papist, a minister of the Free Church, and at the head of the Edinburgh mission to the Irish Papists; and the persons to whom he was propounding questions were Irish papists, with whom he often held these keen discussions, and hundreds of whom were led to give up the missal for the Bible, and the mumbling of the mass for the true worship of God.

From the crowded mission house I passed over to the Gaelic chapel, equally crowded, on the opposite side. They were singing when I entered; and they were *all* singing. And such a shout of hearty devotion I had never heard. Dr. Candlish, very small, very thin, very restless, with a finely-developed head, projecting forehead, and a quick, restless eye, was alone in the pulpit. He laid himself down on the Bible when he prayed. His voice is not well modulated. He preached on the faith of Abraham, with contortions of person and countenance, and of his gown and bands, which were sometimes ludicrous enough. Some of his positions and gestures were almost as awkward, as violent, and as eloquent as were those of Dr. Duff at Exeter Hall. The sermon was abstract and very able, and was heard throughout with fixed attention; but a friend suggested that he put thoughts into the mind of Abraham of which the good old patriarch had never even dreamed. I gave to the suggestion my assent. He is making his mark upon Scotland. Though odd in his manners, which are often abrupt and bluff, he is most affable, and full of conversation. He is a man of great and varied powers.

Nothing more deeply interested me in Edinburgh than the examinations of their schools. On invitation, I went with Dr. Candlish to the examination of the model school of the Free Church, which occupies the house of the good regent, Murray; and where you are shown a thorn-bush planted by Queen Mary, and the room in which the treaty with England was signed. Many of the clergy and of the teachers of the city were there. The examination was thorough, and remarkably well sustained. Never did I hear such an examination in the Shorter Catechism. By boys and girls, ranging from twelve to eighteen or twenty years, it was analyzed with a dexterity and readiness which showed that it was placed on the same ground as algebra, Euclid, grammar, and geography in the science of education. And it is this attention to thorough religious instruction in their youth which has given the Scotch a character for principle and honesty above any other people. After the close of the examination we repaired to the house of Mr. Johnstone, the enterprising publisher, and sat down to dinner with a company of authors, scholars, and teachers, among whom were Dr. Cunningham, Dr. M'Crie, Dr. Hetherington, Dr. Tweedie, Dr. Candlish, names known to fame on both continents, and whose presence would give character to any assemblage. Nothing pertaining to the education of the young is beneath the notice and patronage of Scotland's noblest men. And so it should be in all the earth.

Edinburgh is a city beautiful for situation. In panoramic splendor it is not surpassed by any city of Europe. The solitary grandeur of Arthur's Seat—the castle frowning from its airy height in the midst of the city—Calton Hill, with its observatory, monuments, and unfinished Parthenon, a monument to the pride and poverty of Scotland—the estuary of Forth, expanding into the ocean—the surrounding Pentland, Lammermoor, and Grampian Hills—the picturesque disorder of the Old Town, and the almost painful proportions and elegance of the New, form features of a landscape of great beauty and sublimity. But its true glory lies in its commodious churches, its very able and evangelical ministry, its literary, moral, and religious institutions, and the general intelligence and morality of its people. In all these respects, it stands pre-eminent among the cities of the earth. The world may revile John Knox, and ignorant sectaries may defame the doctrine and order which are distinctively Presbyterian, but Edinburgh and all Scotland present a standing argument in the vindication of both which no mind of ordinary fairness can either gainsay or contradict.

CHAPTER XLII.

Park.—Rev. J. A. James.—Sail to Oban.—Oban.—Royalty in Exile. —Sail round Mull.—Staffa: its Cave.—Iona: its History.—Ruins. —Culdees.—Royal Graves.—The ruling Passion.—Stone Crosses. —Talk on the Wheel-box.

THAT was a pleasant evening which I spent at Park, on the Clyde, the residence of John Henderson, Esquire. It was there I met the Rev. John Angel James, of Birmingham, so widely known for his many pious, evangelical, and greatly useful works. He is very much like his books, pious, elegant, chaste in conversation, very affable, and by no means so English as many of his portraits would represent him. Deeply to my regret, he was prevented, by indisposition, from being my fellow-traveler to the Highlands.

Taking a steamer at Park, we sailed down by Greenock to the Firth of Clyde, and thence by the Kyles of Bute to Loch Fine, and thence by the Crinan Canal through a great many islands up to Oban. The day was calm and warm, and the sail was magnificent, with the Highlands and islands constantly before us, and the scenery changing at every turn. We had on board a large company of hounds and huntsmen, and quite a sprinkling of nobility, on their way to the shooting and hunting grounds in the Highlands. The dogs were the only passengers to whom the nobility paid much attention.

Oban is most pleasantly situated at the head of a small bay. Upon a cliff near the town stands the ivy-clad ruins of Dunolly Castle, the ancient fortress of the MacDougals of Lorn, once a most powerful clan. From the heights above the town are fine views of the sea, of the Isle of Mull, and of many smaller islands, each of which have their spirit-stirring history. It was on these heights I saw, save in the case of soldiers, the only Highland dress I saw in Scotland. And it was worn by a man upward of sixty years of age, of proud bearing, and probably one of the descendants of the "Lords of the Isles." In this Highland village we found the ex-Queen of France, the widow of Louis Philippe, with some of her children, her suite, and her priests. O what a change from Paris to Oban, and from the Tuileries and Versailles to the Caledonia Hotel! Royalty in exile!

We took the steamer early in the morning for Staffa and Iona, those celebrated islands on the western shores of Scotland. The day was bright and calm, and without a ripple on the ocean. On that little island Alexander II. died in 1247, and Haco of Norway met his confederate chieftains. That little island was anciently the residence of the bishops of Argyle. There, on the shores of Mull, is the "Lady Rock," where Maclean exposed his wife to be swept away by the tide; but she was rescued by some of her father's followers. Ignorant of her rescue, Maclean had for her a mock funeral; and was soon afterward put to death by the friends of his injured wife. And there "is woody Morven," famed in the rhapsodies of Ossian. And as we rounded the last promontory of Mull, the islands of which we were in search were seen quietly reposing like sea-birds on the bosom of the Atlantic.

Staffa rises from the ocean straight as a wall, and is of very irregular shape. It is about half a mile square on the top, which is reached with difficulty by means of a ladder. The great attraction of this island is its peculiar basaltic formation, and the "Cave of Fingal." This cave is one of the world's wonders. It is about seventy feet high, thirty-six wide, and recedes inward about two hundred and fifty feet. The entire front and sides are composed of countless basaltic columns, beautifully jointed, and of symmetrical though varied forms. The roof is composed of a rich grouping of overhanging pillars, some of them of snowy whiteness from their calcareous incrustations. The ocean ebbs and flows in this cave, and at full tide boats can go back and forth through its entire length. The columns on the island are sometimes perpendicular, sometimes oblique, and sometimes nearly horizontal. They are generally pentagonal and hexagonal; sometimes they have seven or nine sides; but they are rarely triangular or rhomboidal. Nor are their angles so sharp, nor are the blocks so exquisitely united, as those of the Giant's Causeway, in Ireland. Yet so closely are they often jointed as not to admit between them the blade of a knife.

But neither pencil nor pen can adequately describe this wonder of nature to those who have never seen it. "If this cave were destitute of the order, the symmetry, the richness arising from the multiplicity of parts, combined with the greatness of dimensions and simplicity of style which it possesses; still, the prolonged length, the irregular galleries, the twilight gloom, the echoes of the surge as it rises and falls, the transparent green of the water, and the fairy solitude of the whole scene, can not fail permanently to impress any mind gifted with any sense of beauty in nature or art." And although without inhabitant, without hamlet or hut under which to take shelter from rain or storm, and exposed to every wind that sweeps the sea, it is yet visited yearly by thousands, solely attracted by the wonderful formation and caves of Staffa, where

"Nature itself, it seem'd, would raise
A Minster to her Maker's praise."

After spending some hours amid these wonders, we embarked, and proceeded to Iona, but a few miles distant. Here we went ashore in boats, and were met by a crowd of children, wishing to sell us pebbles and relics of the island. Unlike Staffa, it lies low, possesses a surface of about ten square miles, and has about 400 inhabitants. There is an Established and Free Church, which would seem to indicate a waste of men and money. But we were told that at the disruption, the minister, who yet is on the island, and almost all the people, went out with the Free Church, which rendered the erection of a new church necessary. We here found a circulating library of religious books, kept in a neat room of one of the tenants, who was its librarian, and which was established by Leigh Richmond, on his visit to Iona. What a useful monument to commemorate the visit of that excellent Christian minister.

The great attraction of this island is in its history and ruins. When corruption had deeply infected the Church, and wars and rumors of wars filled all the nations of Europe, a class of religious people fled to this lonely island for the cultivation of religion and letters. These mostly came from Ireland, led by a Christian minister named Columba, and subsequently received the name of Culdees. For ages together they maintained their simple habits and worship, uncorrupted by the errors, and unseduced by the arts and wiles of Popery. This island long continued the great luminary of Scotland and Ireland, and sent out from its narrow domain the men that kept the lamps of religion and learning trimmed and burning in the surrounding islands for many centuries. The Culdees were finally compelled to yield to the all-corrupting power of Rome. At one time they were attacked by the piratical Danes; at another by the Norwegians; and they suffered terribly in the conflicts between the Picts and Scots. In 877 they fled to Ireland. Their abbot was slain, and their monastery pillaged in 985. In 1059 their monastery was consumed. They lingered for nearly a century afterward amid the ruins of their sacred island, when they were scattered over Scotland, and kept the lights of truth burning until the Reformation, which they all hailed as the work of God.

And there before you stand the ruins of their famous old monastery, and of the chapel where these Culdees preached and prayed. The feelings which the first view of them excites is peculiar, after sailing for hours among the barren islands between them and Oban. They rise out of the deep, giving to the desolate region an air of civilization, and stand up a monument to the memory of the pious and holy men whose works yet praise them, though the names of most of them have passed away from the records of men. This was esteemed in Denmark and Norway, as well as in Ireland and Scotland, "an holy island;" and hence you are shown lines of graves of Danish and Scottish kings. On their death they were taken to the "holy isle" for sepulture. In wandering around the ruins, we came to what was obviously the well of the monastery, now almost filled up with rubbish. "What was this?" said a lady of the company. "No doubt the old well of the Culdees," was the reply. "As the Culdees were Baptists, was it not probably their baptistry?" said an intelligent Baptist clergyman from London, who was one of the company. It was the ruling passion strong in Iona. Of the three hundred and sixty-five stone crosses which studded this little isle, but one now remains, which is a rudely-carved pillar twelve or fifteen feet high, and is called the MacLean Cross, after the clan which was once chief among these islands. And as our steamer turned her prow toward Oban, I threw all the emotions of my heart into the sweet words,

"Homeward we turn. Isle of Columba's cell,
Where Christian piety's soul-cheering spark
(Kindled from heaven between the light and dark
Of time) shone like the morning star—farewell."

"You are from America, they tell me," said the captain, as I stood on the wheel-box looking out upon Mull, and straining my eyes to catch a glimpse of Skye. After some conversation as to localities, he again asked, "Did you ever hear of a Bishop Hughes in New York?" After replying in the affirmative, he said, "I was some months ago in Sligo, where I bought a little book called 'Letters to Bishop Hughes, by

Kirwan.' Now I want to know if you have ever seen it or read it?" On replying in the affirmative, he said, "I have read that book over and over; and I have read it to my wife: now I want to ask if you know who Kirwan was?" Without revealing myself to the honest Scot, for which I have since been sorry, I got round the question as well as I could. "Well," said he, as he left me, "I should really like to know how Bishop Hughes could get along with Kirwan." Did I know where to find him, or how to direct it, I would certainly send him a copy of that wonderful production—"Kirwan Unmasked," which has done so much to exalt the literary fame of its author. It affords full proof of his rare qualifications for a high niche in the Dunciad.

CHAPTER XLIII.

To Ballahulish.—Glencoe: its Wildness.—Ossian's Birth-place.—Massacre.—Scotch Bittock.—A Moor.—Barren Possessions.—Duke of Breadalbane.—Loch Lomond.—Sketches from Nature.—Inversnaid.—A Cabin.—Loch Katrine.—Trosachs.—Our Coachman.—Sabbath in Callander.—Identity of the Gaelic and Irish Languages.—Comparison.—To Liverpool.

We took an early start from Oban for Loch Lomond. We sailed up Lochs Linnhe, and Appan, and Levin, which are only salt-water bays, sprinkled all over with barren islands, and were landed at a most miserable village called Ballahulish, where is a very extensive slate quarry. The houses, the women, and the children forcibly recalled some of the villages that we had seen in Connaught. Here we took a stage, and rode at a fearful rate through the celebrated pass of Glencoe, to see which was our object in taking this route This pass or gorge is celebrated for its wildness, and for a fearful massacre perpetrated there in 1691, that leaves a stain upon the character of King William which no effort has been able to remove. The lower portion of it is cultivated; but every sign of cultivation disappears as you advance. Soon you are in a defile, wild to savageness, where you can only see the heavens above you, and ragged rocks on either hand, lifting up their peaks to the clouds. Toward the head of the glen the scenery becomes almost Alpine in rough sublimity; you are reminded of the Alps by the dark shadows of the mountains, and by the wreaths of snow to be seen in all their clefts. Occasionally along the road you see in the piles of stones and sand, and the deep gulleys that interrupt your travel, the fearful power of the mountain torrent; and for some months of the year the scream of the eagle and the roar of these torrents are the only sounds heard in this waste-howling wilderness. The wild stream of Cona rushes through this glen, on the banks of which it is said Ossian was born. Fitting birth-place for a man of such wild fancy!

The Macdonalds of this region were men of desperate character, little less than bandits. They were a powerful clan, both as to number and courage. They were, besides, Jacobites of the worst character, and refused to the last submission to William. At last, however, they took the oath of allegiance, but whether within the prescribed time, or two or three days after, is not so clear. Supposing all was safe, Macdonald dismissed all fear. Two companies of soldiers marched up the glen, quartered among the clan as friends, and, after enjoying their hospitality for nearly two weeks, rose at night, and murdered thirty-eight of them in their beds. It is supposed the criminal party to this tragedy was Breadalbane, between whom and the Macdonalds a long feud existed. "Do you see that green strip of land on the other side of the stream?" said our furious driver. "That is the place where Campbell of Glenlyon murdered the Macdonalds." And we drove on. "There is about a quarter of a mile and a bittock of road here which is very bad; will you walk it, gentlemen?" said the knight of the whip. We all descended; and unless the bittock was six or eight times as long as the quarter, I am mistaken. "How long, driver, did you say it was up that hill?" I inquired, as I mounted to my seat on the top. He pretended not to hear; but he laughed outright when I told him, sweating and puffing, that the next time I walked up that hill, I thought I would ride.

Emerging from this glen, we passed over a moor thirty or forty miles wide, where there was not a habitation visible for many miles. Nothing met the eye but the heath and the mountain, with here and there a stag or a flock of sheep, whose only visible means of support were the stones and the heather. This is the great hunting-ground of the Duke of Breadalbane, whose domains are said to be about sixty miles long. But if all his possessions are like those over which we were passing, he must be poor indeed, for, surely, the more the worse of such lands. In the midst of this wilderness we passed his "shooting-box," said to contain fifty rooms. What, then, must his palace be! We never heard him named but with eulogy, both as to his liberality and humble piety.

We reached Loch Lomond early in the afternoon, and as the boat went down the lake and returned, I resolved to go with her and return, that I might have a full view of the world-famed beauties of these waters.

At its northern extremity, where we embarked, the lake is in form like a canal, not much wider or deeper. Soon the scenery becomes very bold, and the waters expand. Soon there is the appearance of a lake, when the waters spread out into a width of five or six miles.

You pass under the shadow of "the lofty Ben Lomond," and by many pretty islands, and within sight of many sweet summer residences of some of the aristocracy and wealthy merchants of Glasgow; and in about two hours you reach the wharf at its southern point. Thence we retraced our course to Inverarnan, where we spent the night; thus going down and up the lake.

Lomond is the pride of Scottish lakes. It has about thirty islands of very various sizes. On some of these are the ruins of old fortifications; and every island, and projecting rock, and little vale has its history. Under that shelving rock is Rob Roy's cave. That mill stands on the patrimony of Rob; of which, when unjustly deprived, he turned freebooter. That small opening is the entrance to Glen Fruin, where clan Macgregor almost annihilated the Colquhouns, and then murdered about eighty youth who came to see the fight. On that hill was one of the hunting-seats of Fingal. Thus every island, vale, rock, and pass has its bloody history. The sun was setting over Ben Lomond as we were returning—the air was still; the lake from its glassy bosom reflected every shadow that fell upon it. It was the gloaming of a magnificent evening in August, which magnified every object and clothed all nature with an enchanting mellowness. How I wished for the genius of an Angelo, to place on canvas some of the enchanting pictures around me. Under the inspiration of the hour, I absolutely drew out my pencil and commenced sketching from nature. But so rude were my sketches, and so unlike nature, that, ere I left the boat, I gave them to the waters,

"Famous for three things:
Waves without winds,
Fish without fins,
And an island that swims."

Down the lake again to Inversnaid, where we landed for Loch Katrine, five miles distant, and over a very miserable road. I walked up the hill, and, while waiting for a drosky, entered a Highland cabin for inspection. The children could not speak English, but with the mother I held quite a conversation. Two not very clean rooms made up the abode. "Granny," as the young mother called her, lay in the second room upon a bed of straw, one of the most lean and faded old persons I ever saw. I made an effort to speak to her, but she knew only the Gaelic. But there was a Bible with the Psalms on a rude shelf, and the woman was well instructed in religious things. Her church was on the other side of the lake, to which she went every Sunday.

One hour brought us to Loch Katrine, and soon we were on board the smallest edition of a steamer I ever saw, and on the bosom of one of the smallest lakes imaginable. First you are greatly disappointed; but as you proceed, winding about jutting rocks, the scenery grows in beauty, and when you reach the "Trosachs" you are ever more exclaiming how beautiful! The Trosachs is a name given to a space running about three miles, partly on both sides of the lake, consisting of hills and rocks, covered thick with moss and underwood, piled indiscriminately together, and which form a very wild and dark scene. The plot of the "Lady of the Lake" is laid here; and the captain of the tiny steamer shows you the island where Ellen shot her light skiff to the shore—where the "noble gray" died in the chase—and where Roderic Dhu landed. It was certainly pleasing to read the beautiful poem as I did, amid the scenes which it describes; but I could not resist the inference that this loch would be far less interesting if that poem had never been written. The prose and poetry of the lake differ very considerably.

After wandering some hours amid the Trosachs, we took stage to Callander. The road was along small lakes, and glens, and narrow passes, to each and all of which the genius of Scott gave a most romantic history. I was very fortunate in getting a seat by the side of our driver, a fine, burly, intelligent Scotchman, with a red coat and other insignia of office. He seemed to have committed the Lady of the Lake to memory, and as we passed along he would locate the various incidents narrated in it. Here was the gathering-ground of Clan-Alpin—up that mountain the fiery-cross flew. Yonder is the church where the wedding took place—there is the hillside which was covered with men at the sound of Roderic's bugle-horn—there is the glen where was the deadly fight.

> "They tug, they strain! down, down they go;
> The Gael above—Fitz-James below."

And he would spout the passages descriptive of the scenes in right good style, and greatly to our edification and amusement; and when not entirely familiar with passages, he would draw the book from his pocket, holding it in one hand, and guiding his coach and four with the other. But when I learned at Callander that this was a part of his craft to get passengers, my respect for his poetic taste and voluntary rehearsals was greatly diminished. What a pity that a due estimate of the motives so often diminish our regard for the actions of men! What an annoyance, to be always canvassing motives!

I spent the Sabbath in Callander, and mostly with the family of Dr. Cunningham, who was here spending his vacation. The day was a charming one, even for Scotland. Before the hour of service I walked up and down the street, and it was most interesting to see the people streaming into the town in every direction, each with his Bible under his arm. The persons in carriages mostly went to the Established Church, but the vast multitude flocked to the Free. When I entered it, the house was crowded in all its parts. Soon a minister entered the pulpit, in gown and bands, and commenced the service; after which, not an individual entered the house. *All* sang; and the singing was conducted from a desk beneath the pulpit. The whole church was vocal with praise. When the text was announced, all turned to it in their own Bibles. When, in the course of the sermon, a reference was made to Scripture, the people turned to it. Every body seemed attentive, although the sermon was long, and to me dry, though thoroughly evangelical. At the close of the service there was a mutual and kindly recognition of the worshipers, who retired from the town in troops, as they came, each with a Bible under their arm; the most decent, orderly, intelligent, devout class of peasantry that I ever saw, or perhaps that the world knows.

I went to the Established Church in the afternoon, which was in every respect a poor affair. A few persons sat in the gallery, and fewer yet on the first floor.

I sat on a dirty seat, and my feet were on the ground, and a little urchin was playing, through the whole service, among the seats with the stones and gravel. The whole service was in Gaelic, the first I ever heard, and it struck me as unique. The hearers were few, and generally old. The old women wore white high caps without bonnets, and looked exceedingly primitive. The precentor lined the psalm, and sung it; but where he stopped reading and commenced singing, or the contrary, it was difficult to tell, save by the noises of the people around. Worse singing none could desire, and but few could endure. Yet it seemed to the taste of the people, who will suffer no changes in music rendered venerable by being chanted in these fastnesses for three centuries. The sermon was long to me, who could not understand a word of it; but the people hung upon the preacher's lips, who now and then rose up to the region of earnestness. The whole scene—men, women, minister, singing, and all—recalled the earlier worship of the Covenanters; and the life-like representations, in pictures, of that worship can not be fully understood by those who have never seen a Gaelic congregation worshiping in the Highlands. The people before me were the unchanged descendants of their sires. Any of them might be taken for the picture of a Covenanter. The church was very thinly attended, owing partly to the service being in Gaelic, but mainly to the fact that almost all the Highlands have gone with the Free Church.

It is now increasingly evident that the Gaelic and the Irish are the same language. I met with a lady from the Highlands in the Ballinglen school, in Ireland, who, from her knowledge of the Gaelic, read and spoke the Irish fluently. And the Rev. Mr. Brannagan, of the Irish mission, on his first hearing a Gaelic sermon, understood it perfectly; and, on a visit to Callander, he found no difficulty in conversing with persons in Gaelic who did not understand English. This may lead to most important results in the efforts now making to evangelize Ireland. The identity of language opens a wide field for missionaries from the Highlands.

In Scotland the churches are far plainer than with us. Those of Drs. Candlish, Gordon, and Guthrie, of Edinburgh, the most fashionable there, are not to be compared with our best class of churches. The same is true of the churches in England and Ireland. They seem to go upon the principle, which has too much evidence to substantiate it, that gay churches, gay people, and lax doctrine and discipline, go together. The preaching is simple and scriptural, and far more earnest than with us, but not so well arranged or digested. But their congregations far surpass ours in earnest worship. The heartlessness and frivolity often seen in American churches I never witnessed in any Protestant congregations abroad. I have not a doubt but that the Presbyterianism of Scotland is the purest, the truest, the most spiritual type of Christianity known among men.

My time for homeward voyage was drawing nigh, and delay was no longer possible; and I was away from Callander, through Stirling to Edinburgh; and from the Athens of the North, through Lanark, Lockerbie, to Gretna; and through Carlisle and Preston to Liverpool, where I rested for a few days, enjoying the hospitality of dear Christian friends while finishing my preparations for home.

CHAPTER XLIV.

To Wales.—Menai Straits.—Tubular Bridge.—Length.—View from beneath: from the Top.—Last View.—Friends at Liverpool.—Sailing.—Voyage.—Passengers.—Last Evening.—Our Farewell.

By an old and kind friend, now making his mark in the commercial circles of Liverpool, a visit was projected for me to Wales, and to the Britannia Bridge, famous in all the earth as a work of art. The Rev. Mr. Roberts, a Dissenting clergyman, was my companion. We passed through old Chester, visiting its Cathedral, its Roman wall, Holywell, St. Asaph's, Conway to Bangor, near to which are the famous suspension and tubular bridges. During this ride on the Chester and Holyhead railway, the mountains of Wales, propping the skies, were on one side of us, and the sea, white with canvas, on the other. We stopped at the bridge, and after the effect of our astonishment so far subsided as to permit us to go on, we went *under* it, and *through* it, and *over* it.

The Menai Straits is an arm of the sea, separating the Isle of Anglesea from the main land, through which the waters of the Irish Sea and of St. George's Channel rush with great force. In this channel, and between very high banks, the tide rises nearly thirty feet, and the waters are eternally vibrating in a current, whether in or out, of from seven to ten miles an hour. The question to be solved was, how the railway connecting Dublin by Holyhead with London, could be carried over these straits? And the question was solved by the erection of this wonderful bridge, far more wonderful than the Pyramids of Egypt. I will attempt a brief description of it.

On either side of the straits are built vast abutments, and rising about two hundred feet from amid the waters are three vast tapering towers; and upon these abutments and towers the vast iron tubes are laid, through which heavily-laden railway trains are whistling almost every hour of the day. The length of this tube is but a little less than two thousand feet; while its two main spans, reaching over the deepest waters, are each four hundred and sixty feet. Through this tube there is a double track, and so firmly is it constructed that it scarcely vibrates when a heavily-laden train is flying through it.

You are amazed as you look up from the waters upon the stupendous structure hanging in the air above you, and when you see long trains of cars flying in at the one side and flying out at the other! And you are amazed, when you pass through it, at the genius which contrived it, and at the skill which executed it. But your amazement rises into rhapsody as you ascend to the top of the tube and walk over its extreme length. Beneath you the cars are flying laden with passengers, and in the waters yet farther beneath you ships are sailing with all their canvas flying. I was in the air above while several vessels of three or four hundred tons burden passed beneath. On one side of you the famous Suspension Bridge hangs in the air, over which carriages and wagons are passing, which in the distance seem to have nothing to sustain them. On another side is seen reposing in beauty the marble castle of the Marquis of Anglesea, on a green lawn sloping to the water, and shaded with trees of unknown age. East and west are seen the glittering waters of the Irish Sea and St. George's Channel; while the southern horizon is bounded by the hills of Caernarvon, among which the patriarch Snowdon lifts his bold and rugged head to the clouds.

It was enough. We descended. And as we walked toward Bangor, we felt in kind as we did when taking our last view of St. Peter's and of the glorious Alps.

It was truly refreshing to meet in Liverpool Mrs. Mary Lundy Duncan, whom I left in America, whose literary labors are so excellent and useful, and whose visit to our country will not be soon forgotten by those who had the privilege and pleasure of making her acquaintance. Having seen her in my own house, she gave me a home feeling whenever I met her, which was almost daily during my sojourn.

The day of our departure was come. At noon we left Prince's wharf for the noble steamer Atlantic, which lay in the river. Mrs. Duncan and other dear friends accompanied us to the ship. Soon Captain West took his stand on the wheel-house, and ordered all, save passengers, ashore. It was a tender hour. Some were parting to meet no more this side of the grave; and they so felt. Soon our wheels were in motion. We waved handkerchiefs to the dear friends we were leaving as long as we could distinguish them. As Liverpool and New Brighton died away behind us, we turned our eyes to the scenes that were before us. Soon we passed the Skerries and Holyhead. Soon the rock-bound shore of Erin rose to view; and soon, leaving Cape Clear behind us, we were out on the broad bosom of the sea. Our passengers were numerous, and of every variety. There were ministers, physicians, editors, lawyers, merchants, farmers, mechanics, and play-actors. Some were well, and some were very ill bred persons. Nor did it take either long to show their nature. Some were returning from the "World's Fair," which had attractions for all kinds of people, and our captain had never a more miscellaneous company. With the usual attendants on a voyage, such as head winds, high and smooth seas, sea-sickness, the usual alternations between eating, drowsing, and sleeping, we pursued our course, our wheels never ceasing for a moment to revolve until we entered the Bay of New York.

Our last evening on board was the evening of the Sabbath. We had taken a pilot, and our noble captain resigned his noble ship to his care. We meet in the cabin for evening service. The closing address was from the words "Finally, brethren, farewell." And as we commended each other in prayer to God, and implored the protection of Heaven upon our ship and her commander through all their future voyages, the deepest solemnity pervaded the entire company. And as we sung a parting hymn, every bosom swelled with emotion, and many eyes were overflowing with tears. We retired; and when we awoke in the morning, the Atlantic lay quietly at her pier.

THE END.

www.ingramcontent.com/pod-product-compliance
Lightning Source LLC
LaVergne TN
LVHW010213110826
845151LV00004B/1071

9781425528188